GERMAN
MILITARY
INTELLIGENCE

'The Big Three' of the Abwehr: Canaris (*centre*) with his two
chief subordinates, Lahousen and Piekenbrock in Russia, 1942.

GERMAN MILITARY INTELLIGENCE

Paul Leverkuehn

PRAEGER – NEW YORK

BOOKS THAT MATTER

Published in the United States of America in 1954
by Frederick A. Praeger, Inc., Publishers, 105 West 40th Street,
New York 18, N.Y.

Translated from the German by
R. H. Stevens and Constantine FitzGibbon

Library of Congress Catalog Card Number 54–11544

Printed in Great Britain by
EBENEZER BAYLIS AND SON LTD.
Worcester

CONTENTS

CONTENTS

LIST OF ILLUSTRATIONS

1

A German Intelligence Officer in Istanbul

THE German Military '*Nachrichtendienst*' corresponds broadly to what, in the English-speaking world, is understood by 'Intelligence Service'; while the term *Abwehr* (literally 'Defence)' was originally applied to that particular branch of the Nachrichtendienst which had the task of combating the activities of foreign intelligence services; in other words, it meant the German Counter-Espionage Section.

When the hundred thousand-strong army permitted to Germany under the Versailles Treaty was formed on January 21st, 1921, an 'Abwehr Section' was set up in the German Ministry of Defence in Berlin. This Abwehr Section was under the command of Colonel Gempp, who had worked in the German Intelligence Service during the first war under Colonel Nicolai. The Section was a small one and consisted of two or three General Staff Officers with a round half-dozen officers and a small clerical establishment attached; it was divided into two Sub-Sections—East and West—but originally it possessed no technical facilities for such things as wireless, the preparation of passports, personal documents and the like, which are essential to the efficient working of a service of this nature. For out-station work it had at its disposal the Abwehr stations which had been set up in each of the seven military commands and which initially consisted of one General Staff Officer, one officer assistant and such clerical staff as was required. It was gradually expanded to include offensive as well as defensive intelligence work, both within Germany and abroad, but from that time the term Abwehr has remained in accepted use.

1

Individual undertakings of the Abwehr Service have been the subject of innumerable stories in the press. They are based partly on information given by those who took part in them. But this information has often been supplemented and embellished with fictitious dialogue and other ornaments until it is hard to see where truth ends and fiction begins. On the other hand, to those who urge that a proper history of the Abwehr Service ought to be written, the usual reply has so far been that the files of the Abwehr have been taken to Washington by the Americans and are therefore no longer available. But the importance of these files must not be exaggerated, any more than that of the Canaris Diaries, about which so much has recently been published. Much of the Abwehr's most significant activity finds no place in the official files.

In the out-stations we burnt, with a certain measure of satisfaction, everything that had been committed to paper, and quite apart from the obligation to do so, we were only too glad to be rid of it. The contents of the captured files are only the dead bones of the story; the living spirit survives in the memories of those who served, and when they are dead, then the history of the Abwehr can no longer be written.

To set down some of the stories of the men who served in the Abwehr is the thought which gave impetus to the writing of this book. I have, of course, asked myself whether I can accept the responsibility for its publication, and I feel justified in giving myself an affirmative answer. In the first place, as Chief of the Istanbul Station and also of the branch of the intelligence service called the Near East War Organization (1941–44), I acquired practical experience of Abwehr activity; I knew Admiral Canaris, for many years head of the Abwehr, personally and had ample opportunity to observe both the work of Abwehr Headquarters and his direction of it. On the other hand, as a reserve officer, I was sufficiently detached from its activities to maintain an objective attitude. Furthermore, as defending counsel for the Supreme Headquarters Staff at Nuremberg and for Field-Marshal von Manstein at Hamburg, I later had to grapple with the problems that confronted the High Command and thus obtained an insight into the actions of German military leaders which was essential to a proper evaluation of the place of the Abwehr Service within the whole of Germany's war organization.

It has not been possible, nor was it ever my intention, to write a complete history, to deal with every phase of the war in every land in which the Abwehr operated. Such a work would be altogether too comprehensive, and far too exhausting for the general reader. Rather I have tried to select the most important or typical episodes. What is here described is based on absolutely authentic information. That I have not been able to do full justice to the accomplishments of all my brother officers is a fact which I must record with regret.

I have, in most cases, omitted or changed the names of those men who kindly helped me in the production of this book, due primarily to the fact that every member of any intelligence service has a not unnatural aversion to finding his name in print, for all the world to see. Not a few of the members of the Abwehr, too, have had bitter experiences in the post-war period, and therefore prefer to remain anonymous. I have fully respected both the wishes of the former and my obligations towards the latter; but to all who gave me their invaluable support I wish to express my heartfelt thanks.

At the outbreak of war in 1939, the Near and Middle East were of no direct interest to the German High Command, and it was not for a moment considered likely that German troops would be called upon to operate in these parts of the world. They were, however, of indirect interest, because of the pact with Soviet Russia. Germany had been compelled to come to an agreement with the Russians on the division of Poland and to cede to them both Finland and the Baltic States as spheres of influence. This was, admittedly, regrettable, but it did not threaten to have any warlike repercussions which would affect Germany directly; and from the point of view of German war industry and economy, these countries were of no importance. There was but one spot which aroused apprehension—Rumania. A war in the Balkans would make things very uncomfortable, and if the Rumanian oilfields were lost or came under Russian control, then Germany would be entirely dependent for her natural oil supplies on Russia. It was known that the Russians intended to occupy and annex Bessarabia. In an attempt to distract them from this it was considered whether it would not be possible to persuade them to turn their activities to the Near or Middle East—or perhaps even further eastwards. An onslaught on Afghanistan and a threat to the North-West frontier of India would, from the German point of view, have been an excellent thing, for it would have tied down very large British forces which otherwise could be sent to a European theatre of war. This Afghan idea, however, was quickly abandoned as I shall show in a later chapter.

Attention was next turned to the possibilities open to Russian forces debouching from the Caucasus. Here, there appeared to be two possible fields of activity. They could either advance in to the plains of Mesopotamia and attack the Mosul oilfields, or they could thrust southwards through Persia and seize the oil-wells of the Anglo-Iranian Oil Company.

But these projects also proved, on examination, to be impracticable. An advance through Persia would have called for a far greater effort than that which would be required for the occupation of Bessarabia; and in examining the possibilities of an attack on Mesopotamia, the presence of the French Army in Syria under General Weygand obviously became a consideration of primary importance. Any action by the Russians would undoubtedly have led to immediate intervention by these French forces, and it was doubtful whether the Russians, far from feeling themselves capable of indulging in military adventures in this direction, did not regard Weygand's army as constituting a dangerous threat to themselves. About this latter army very little was known. It was estimated to consist of between a hundred and a hundred and fifty thousand men, but information on its composition was as meagre as was that on its armament. At the turn of the year 1939–40, when the Russo-Finnish War almost led to hostilities between Russia and the Anglo-French Allies, the High Command was much pre-occupied with the possible future role of Weygand's army. While it was thought that it would probably intervene in the Balkans, the possibility could not entirely be dismissed that it might be used for a forced march on Baku and the seizure of its oilfields. If the latter course were adopted, a very dangerous situation would arise, for at that time Baku was still Russia's chief source of oil, a very large proportion of which was earmarked for export to Germany, and the German High Command was dependent on these supplies for the prosecution of the war.

Information was meagre, too, on the nature of the terrain which lay between Weygand's army and Baku. The French, obviously, could move freely within their own mandated territory, which in the main consisted of desert and in the east stretched as far as the Tigris; and beyond the Tigris they had the North Persian road which the British had constructed after the first war. But then they would come face to face with the Kara Dagh mountains. This was the crucial point, and whether any roads existed through the Kara Dagh capable of taking military traffic could not be deduced from any of the maps available.

In the first war the Scheubner-Richter expedition had operated in this district during the winter of 1915–16. I was the last living survivor of this expedition and thus the only officer of the *Wehrmacht* who had ever seen field service in North Persia. The Chief of the Armed Forces Division at Supreme Headquarters, Colonel Warlimont, urgently requested Admiral Canaris to send me on a military reconnaissance of Azerbaijan, with instructions at the same time to find out as much as I could about the strength and combat effectiveness of the Weygand army. I was appointed Consul in Tabriz, and in March 1940 I set out to take up my appointment.

I very quickly established the fact that a road through the

Kara Dagh mountains existed which was capable of carrying mountain troops, and I came to the conclusion that two mobile divisions, composed and armed for mountain warfare, would be able to reach Baku and remain there long enough to destroy it. Serious Russian resistance could not be counted upon; the Russians were suffering from the consequences of the war with Finland, and the Russian Army, thanks to the purges of the 1930s, in which the High Command had been well nigh decimated, and from which it had never recovered, was still severely handicapped.

This North Persian reconnaissance was not, of course, confined merely to an examination of the road communications available between Baku and Tabriz, but also included a survey of all the possibilities for the movement of troops in this area. It became obvious that nobody, British or anybody else, had given the matter a thought. There were a few large-scale maps, but for the most part I had to base my travels on the 1 : 1,000,000 International Map of the World. On it numerous blanks represented vast areas which had never been explored, and what was shown on the map proved to be largely inaccurate.

The road from the Turkish frontier via Khoi Tabriz to Teheran was part of the ancient silk route which ran from Central Asia to the Black Sea near Trebizond—one of the classical thoroughfares of history; but even of this route no military reconnaissance had ever been made To the south-east of Tabriz is the Shibli pass, which is of considerable military importance. A little further south is the so-called Kaflankuh gorge, through which the road winds for many miles beside a rushing torrent. Both these features form obstacles of primary importance, but neither of them was shown on the map.

I found, too, that the ambitious plans of the old Shah, Reza Pahlevi, to construct a road parallel to the frontier from Tabriz through Kurdistan to the south had petered out while still in the initial preparatory stage. Such a road would have been of decisive military importance; it would further have been of use for the pacification of the Kurdish tribes in these mountainous districts; but this, as I found out on the spot, was very far from having been accomplished.

I had heard that on the orders of the Shah the Skoda Works had built a modern bridge near Sakkis, to the south of Lake Urmia, and that fifteen miles or so further south still there were two more new bridges. The road to Sakkis was fit for motor traffic, and the district therefore was approachable to motorized units.

In Sakkis there was indeed a magnificent concrete bridge, but it was never used, for the people preferred to cross by the neighbouring ford, as their fathers had done for centuries before them. I wanted to go on another fifteen miles to see the other two bridges; however I now met with determined resistance from my interpreter and chauffeur. During a pause for lunch at Mehshad they had done a little sightseeing and in an open place they had discovered a gallows, from which two Kurds were hanging, who had been executed for highway robbery. Now a motor-car was something of a rarity in these parts and could certainly be regarded most gratefully as an ideal object for attack. One shot in the tyres would suffice to bring it to a standstill, and it was the prospect or the premonition of such a possibility which led to the chauffeur's firm refusal to go on any further. Nor was he altogether wrong; on that very day a car was attacked in the Shibli pass, one occupant was killed and the other two were wounded. And one of the perpetrators confessed afterwards that the attack had been intended for the German Consul!

German successes in the French campaign removed any danger which might have threatened from the Weygand army. Weygand himself was recalled to France, and his army in Syria was included in the general terms of the armistice. Of some interest is the question—was the whole undertaking superfluous, or did the Allies ever really consider the possibility of an onslaught on Baku? During the campaign in France the secret files of the French General Staff fell into German hands. From them it appears that just at the time when the General Staff of the Wehrmacht was voicing its anxiety about Baku to Admiral Canaris in January 1940, the French Premier, Daladier, directed General Gamelin, the Chief of the General Staff, and Admiral Darlan, the Chief of the Naval Staff, to examine the possibilities of carrying out an attack on Baku; and these two officers in their turn consulted the British. It is characteristic of the difference between the Allied and the German ways of thinking that while the former decided to plan for a combined sea and air operation, the Germans approached the problem as one purely for the land forces. It was quite obvious that the possibility of employing the army had never even been considered by the Allies; had they done so, some traces of the preliminary reconnaissance which they would have had to make would have come to light. Pre-requisites to a combined sea and air operation, however, were, first, that the Dardanelles should be opened, and secondly, that the Turks would give permission for flying over Turkish terri-tory, the granting of which would have been tantamount to an abandonment of Turkish neutrality. It is rather remarkable that a straightforward land operation, involving nothing more than a march through Iraq and Persia, should not even have been considered, and that instead an expedition should have been planned, which must encounter the gravest possible political obstacles.

Meanwhile the results of the reconnaissance which I had undertaken were not without some value to the Abwehr. When the German Armies reached the Caucasus and planted their flag on the Elbrus in 1942, the Mosul oilfield and the great Anglo-Iranian installations on the Karun river looked very close indeed. It was assumed that the German Armies would advance upon them. It was also assumed that the British would destroy their refineries and wells, in the same way that they had destroyed other important sources of military supplies when forced to retreat. Since this refinery and these wells were vital to the oil supply of Europe, the Abwehr was set the task of evolving a plan which would prevent such destruction.

The assumption was that before they retired the British would unseal the borings and render the refinery useless by demolition. Such measures, in the opinion of experts, would put the South Iran oilfields out of action for many years to come; new borings would have to be sunk in the vicinity of the old wells, while the refinery would have to be completely rebuilt. A technically completely novel plan was therefore evolved—the *système d'ensablement*—the 'sanding-up technique'—whereby the refinery and the wells were to be put temporarily out of action while still in the possession of the British; in other words, an attempt was to be made to sabotage an act of sabotage This technique, in simple terms, envisaged the filling of borings, wells, derricks, conduit pipes, etc., with sand, which would go a long way towards counteracting the unsealing of the one and the demolition of the others. The project was at first condemned as quite fantastic in Berlin; but its authors persisted and succeeded in getting the plan submitted to a panel of experts who, after meticulous examination, pronounced it technically feasible.

On this, detailed planning was immediately started. It was decided that the enterprise should be carried out by a group of acknowledged experts, under the leadership of a man who was well acquainted, not only with the refinery and the oilfields, but also with the country and the people, and particularly with the Sheikhs of the marsh Arab tribes, which provided most of the employees at the oilfields. The plan was making steady progress, but it had to be abandoned when the German advance in the Caucasus was brought to a halt and when subsequent battles made it apparent that the Caucasian mountains marked the limit to any further penetration in that direction.

At the beginning of 1941 the Abwehr sent Major Schulze-Holthus to replace me as Consul in Tabriz. When the British and the Russians invaded Persia in August 1941, he and his wife, together with the other Germans, were at first interned in Shimrau, near Teheran; from there, however, they escaped, and after an adventurous journey they found refuge with the Kashgais, one of the warlike tribes of South Persia. In order to re-establish contact with Germany, Frau Schulze-Holthus went in

B

disguise over the Kurdish mountains into Turkey—a bold and strenuous undertaking. The Security Service (the *Sicherheitsdienst* or S.D., the Nazi Party secret service) sent two men to join Schulze-Holthus, and the small group stood their ground until the Kashgais, surrounded by the British, handed them over. Schulze-Holthus has described his experiences in an excellent book; there remains therefore nothing to add here, except to say that his attitude and behaviour were in every way exemplary and worthy of an Abwehr officer. Far away and cut-off from his superiors he showed both courage and imagination of a high order, and he made the utmost of the possibilities inherent in his position. Nor did his efforts go unrewarded; he tied down a number of British troops, the forces and material which the enemy had to bring into action were considerable, and around this solitary man a complete little theatre of war was developed.

Although no further reconnaissance of the Near or Middle East was for the moment demanded on behalf of the armed forces, the Abwehr found new fields of activity there in January 1941.

The impetus thereto did not originate in Abwehr circles, but from the Foreign Office, primarily at the insistence of the former Minister in Baghdad, Doctor Grobba. At that time Rashid Ali el Gailani, one of the leaders of the anti-British party, was Prime Minister of Iraq, and his great opponent was Nuri Pasha Said, who in the first war had helped Lawrence to seize the Arab territories from the Turks. Rashid Ali considered that the war in Europe offered him an excellent opportunity to rid Iraq of British influence, and in his plans he was supported by the Mufti of Jerusalem, Haj Amin el Husseini, the President of the Pan-Islamic Congress. He was also counting on German assistance, and this was promised him. Each party to the agreement, however, was soon to be disappointed in the other; the Germans had assessed far too highly the military efficiency of the Iraqi troops which Rashid Ali was able to put in the field, while Rashid Ali and the Mufti had greatly exaggerated ideas on the

10

amount of help that Germany was in a position to give them. A few odd aircraft were sent, but they were by themselves of no combat value, and their cargo was far too insignificant to be of the slightest practical use to the Iraquis. The rebellion collapsed quickly. It cost a few German officers their lives, and Rashid Ali and the Mufti fled to Teheran. The Germans attempted, through Doctor Rahn, to obtain support for the rebellion, or at least facilities and assistance for the German lines of supply, from the French troops in Syria; but at that time Franco-German relations had not yet reached the requisite state of cordiality.

The rebellion in Baghdad nevertheless showed that this part of the world might well become of interest to the German High Command, and Admiral Canaris decided to open increased Intelligence activities, either in Turkey or from bases in that country. A War Organization, which was the name given to an intelligence centre in a neutral, Allied, or occupied country, was established in the German Embassy in Ankara, a subsidiary station was set up in Istanbul, and Canaris himself, accompanied by Piekenbrock, his righthand man, paid a visit to Turkey early in August 1941.

Direction of the War Organization was entrusted initially to Major, later Lieut.-Colonel, Meyer-Zermatt, who previously had been the Director of the War Organization in the Netherlands, and I myself was put in charge of the subsidiary station in Istanbul. As Ankara was purely a governmental town and administrative centre, and therefore very easy to supervise, it was obvious that most of the practical work would have to be carried out from Istanbul.

I took up my duties in July 1941. Beyond an order to set up an Intelligence organization for the reconnaissance of the Near and Middle East, I received no instructions of any kind. Three empty rooms were placed at my disposal, but personnel I had none. As a start, I bought a desk, three chairs, a cabinet and a typewriter. The latter was not of much use for the moment as I, unfortunately, had never learnt to type, but I hoped I would soon find someone who could, and, in any case, some little time must elapse before there would be any reports to send in.

My first recruit knew no shorthand and typed with one finger, but she possessed some other, quite exceptional, qualities. This was Paula Koch who, after the war, was introduced to a goggling public by the illustrated press as 'the Mata Hari of the second world war'. The analogy is poor in the extreme; Mata Hari was a somewhat flighty young woman from Paris, while Paula Koch was a devout Catholic who in the first world war had been in charge of the most advanced dressing-station of the army which, under General von Kress had advanced to the banks of the Suez Canal. 'She has gained a permanent place in the history of that war,' one General Staff Officer said of her, and no account of the Suez Canal campaign has been written which does not at least mention her name.

She had grown up in Aleppo. After the first war she had established one hospital in Pernambuco and another in the Dutch East Indies, and in the early days of the second war she had devoted herself to the care of the Germans interned in Syria. In her parents' home in Aleppo she had got to know all those Germans who were of any importance in the Near East and was on friendly terms with most of the great Arab families. Through her good offices I established contact with the Arab emigrants in Istanbul, the ablest of whom was Musa Husseini, the nephew and heir-presumptive to the Mufti of Jerusalem. He had studied in London and at El Azar in Cairo, the greatest Islamic academy in the world, and his friendly relationships stretched from one end of the Arab world to the other.

About this time his uncle's friend and brother conspirator, Rashid Ali el Gailani, appeared in Istanbul. To have anything to do with him was a matter of some delicacy for the Ambassador, for the Turks intensely disliked the Germans to have any dealings with the Arabs; they preferred to retain in their own hands all relations with these recalcitrant subjects of theirs, as they were wont to call them. The Ambassador was glad, therefore, to leave it to me, as Assistant Military Attaché and Head

12

of the Abwehr station, to maintain relations with Rashid Ali. This contact opened the doors into all the Arab countries; when a little later an exiled Egyptian Prince threw in his lot with us, Egypt, too, was drawn into the network of our Intelligence activities; by means of contacts with Russian emigrants living in Istanbul a measure of observation on Russia also became possible. First and foremost among the latter was a Menshevik who in 1919 had been a member of the Government of the independent republic of Georgia in Tiflis, and whose advice was invaluable.

When the Russians and the British occupied North and South Persia respectively, in August 1941, the Germans were of course driven out of that country. But neither trade nor the pilgrim traffic ceased; and as the Shiahs went on their pilgrimages either to Karbela, south of Baghdad, or to Meshed in the eastern corner of North Persia, every devout pilgrim had to travel through the whole of the Russian and part of the British occupied zones; and this he was quite willing to do, particularly if helped on his way with a little cash. But he only got the money, admittedly, on condition that he kept his eyes and ears open.

All these nationally-minded persons had, of course, first to be carefully trained for military intelligence duties. Their own interests were purely political, and so Istanbul very soon became the centre of a political intelligence service as well. Towards the latter many of our Turkish friends were also attracted. The Turks were primarily concerned with the preservation of their country's neutrality. The long tradition of Turco-German military collaboration, which began as long ago as the days of Frederick the Great, made it natural for the Turks to talk more openly to Germans than to other Europeans; and they became all the more communicative when they thought that their information might make some contribution towards showing the Germans how to end the war by political agreement.

The Turkish Foreign Service has an impressive tradition, and even to-day it is still obvious that it once served an Empire which stretched from the Persian Gulf to the gates of Vienna. The reports of the Turkish Missions in the various Allied capitals were always most interesting. The British made the task of the German Intelligence Service easier by not always treating the Turks with the respect to which these proud people felt themselves entitled. British policy towards Turkey during the nineteenth century had been based on the principle of support and protection for the Christian minorities *vis-à-vis* Islam. It was Gladstone who coined the phrase 'the unspeakable Turk' and had demanded his expulsion from Europe 'bag and baggage'. The Turk, however, being a proud man, reacts sharply if he feels that he is regarded as inferior to the Armenian, the Jew or the Greek. One of my most fruitful sources of information was a Turk who was employed by a British firm, the United Kingdom Commercial Corporation, but had been passed over in promotion in favour of members of these minorities.

It is a very common fallacy that information can easily be bought for money. Actually, this is very seldom so, at any rate in the Orient. Some other motive must usually be present, and hatred and revenge are amongst the most reliable of the allies of an intelligence service. Once, in connection with something which admittedly had nothing to do with intelligence, I desired to find out how big a bribe a local British Intelligence Officer had paid to a certain lawyer, and I was very anxious to have a peep at the relevant file which was kept in the British Consulate General. Within three days it was on my desk. (The sum, incidentally, was far greater than anything I could have afforded.) The file went safely back, and it had not cost me a farthing to get a look at it. The explanation is this: a relative of one of the employees of the Consulate General had been killed by an Englishman, and this was quite enough to ensure that any insight I required into British Consulate affairs was immediately forthcoming.

From the beginning I regarded my mission more as a politico-military than as a purely military task. The most important question, I told myself, was whether the Turks, who were allied to the British, would abandon their neutrality and enter the war against Germany. That they would do this of their own free will was unlikely in the extreme; but under pressure they might well be compelled to do so. Such pressure could come only from Syria and from Iraq against South Turkey. It was therefore vital to find out the strength of the British and Free French forces in those countries, and this could easily be done by systematic observation, the results of which could be considerably supplemented by information from Cairo, the centre of allied activity in the Middle East.

Traffic between Egypt and Turkey was not interrupted during the war. The Egyptian royal house was of Turkish origin; Mehmed Ali, the founder of the Egyptian dynasty, was born in Kavalla. Up to the time of the first war the ruler of Egypt styled himself the Khedive—which means the Representative, for he was the Viceroy of the Khalif, who resided in Constantinople. When he assumed the title of King, the close social relationship between Constantinople and Cairo continued to flourish, and many Egyptian families, whose presence in Egypt was not welcome to the British, retired to Istanbul; to obtain information from them and thus from their relations and friends who had remained in Egypt was easy.

Direct reconnaissance in the area to the south of the Turkish frontier was carried out partly by simple visual observation—finding out the numbers of troops, noting troop movements, recording the signs and badges on military vehicles. We were, however, compelled to give our Arab collaborators some instruction, designed both to curb oriental fantasy as regards numbers and to teach them to reproduce such emblems and badges as they observed in a recognizable form. This was fairly simple when it was a question of St. George mounted on his charger or some other readily recognizable symbol. But it became a little more difficult when Australian and New Zealand units arrived, wearing as badges animals which the Arabs had never seen in their lives, such as a kangaroo; and a kangaroo is an even more astonishing looking beast when drawn by an

Arab observer than it is in real life! For such instruction I was lucky enough to have the services of a Professor of Oriental Studies who had been trained on the General Staff, together with the former head of the language section of a Turkish college, both with a few assistants. This instructional cadre worked with the precision and conscientiousness of a General Staff unit and achieved excellent results.

As passage through the Mediterranean was very restricted, the British found themselves compelled to send most reinforcements for Egypt and for the Ninth and Tenth Armies in Syria around the Cape and through the Red Sea. The British assembly area was Egypt itself. A considerable proportion of newly arrived units and stores was, however, concentrated in Syria and Palestine. The information gathered by my organization was collated by Foreign Armies, West, the relevant intelligence section at Supreme Army Headquarters and then passed on to Headquarters, Africa Corps. For nearly two years the routine work of my station consisted in the preparation of situation and troop-distribution maps, the reporting of the arrival and probable employment of motorized and armoured formations, the distribution of, and reinforcements to, R.A.F. stations, and the collection of information of general military interest which was of direct concern to the North African theatre of operations. We reported, for example, the sinking of the British battleship H.M.S. *Barham* forty-six hours after it had occurred. This had neither been admitted by the British, nor had it been found out by Naval Intelligence, or observed by any of our troops in North Africa. The elimination of a capital ship of this size had, as will be readily appreciated, a very vital bearing on the naval operations in the Mediterranean. The loss of the *Barham* was only admitted by the British three months later.

Contact with Arab circles and its maintenance made considerable demands on us. This interesting task was centred for some time around Rashid Ali, the Iraqi Prime Minister, who had fled to Turkey, while the Mufti had remained in Teheran. When the Germans and Italians were driven out of Persia, the latter attached himself to the Italian Ambassador, disguised as a footman, and as a result of the protection thus afforded to him he had no choice but to go to Rome. When Rashid Ali heard this, he became jealous and demanded to be sent to Berlin. This was by no means simple. He had given his word of honour to the Turkish Government that he would not leave the country, but the latter, not relying wholly on this parole, watched him very closely. In this way they were not only supported by the British, but the probability is that the Russians, too, kept a pretty strict eye on him.

How, anyway, to get him out of the country was a problem in itself. It would be quite easy to procure the necessary German passport, but it was found impossible to insert the requisite particulars regarding his arrival and sojourn in Turkey. In the Consulate General were lying the results of the excavations made by an archæological expedition. It would not have been very difficult to ship one of the bigger of these cases to Bulgaria. The Security Service man, who was working on the problem with me, had one of them prepared, and Rashid Ali expressed his willingness to travel in it. Even so, it was by no means a simple business.

Then the Foreign Office came to our help. The Turkish Government had invited a German press delegation to pay a visit. It arrived in Istanbul in the Foreign Minister's private aircraft and brought with it a great case, big enough and strong enough to harbour a grown man, though alternative means had also been prepared. The Turkish Government had been told that the German delegation would consist of eight members, and when the aircraft arrived, eight passports, sure enough, were produced for inspection. The holder of the eighth passport, Herr Wackernagel, like the other members of the delegation, received an invitation to dine with the Turkish Press Club that same evening. To the lively regret of the German delegation and their Turkish hosts, Herr Wackernagel could not accept, as he had been taken suddenly and seriously ill. He was also quite unfit to undertake the journey to Ankara, on which the delegation set off the next day. The festivities lasted for several days. On the evening before the party was due to return to Germany, Rashid Ali arrived at the Consulate General. It had required the most careful preparations so to arrange his movements between his country house in Erinkoi on the Sea of Marmora and his town residence that for twenty-four hours he would be able to elude the vigilant watch of the Turks, the British and the Russians.

When he arrived, a German doctor was informed that Herr Wackernagel was in need of medical attention. Rashid Ali was handsomely muffled in bandages which would have looked well on a mumps patient. Fortunately, he was able to sleep peacefully, but early the next morning he had to be thoroughly bandaged up again, and he arrived at the airport in a state of collapse which aroused the sympathetic pity of all who saw him. The waves of enthusiasm and alcohol had run so high the previous evening that only a very few Turks had turned up to say their farewells, and their one idea was to get back home as quickly as they could.

After the war I had the chance of asking a member of the British Intelligence Service what the British had reported to London about Rashid Ali's escape. The report London received stated that Rashid Ali had escaped by ship to Bulgaria, and the original report was later confirmed from a reliable source. This was exactly the story which had been deliberately put out by the Istanbul Abwehr station.

The Turkish Foreign Minister complained bitterly to the German Ambassador about Rashid Ali's behaviour. With scornful contempt he cried out: 'The fellow broke his parole!' And this, undoubtedly, was perfectly true.

The other members of the Arab emigrant community were regarded very differently by the Turks. Musa Husseini did not have to escape; on the contrary, he was told that he was a public nuisance and must leave the country, and there was no alternative open to him but to make for Germany. Before this happened, however, he did agree to one more small enterprise with his friends in Syria, and he came and urged me to support a political revolt in that country. This I refused to do, because political activity did not at that time come within the terms of reference of the Istanbul Abwehr station. But I did agree that Berlin Headquarters should put certain means at his disposal, if any material of military intelligence importance should be forthcoming. Our argument centred on what an enterprise of this sort would cost, and in the end, after much precise reckoning, we came to the conclusion that the expenses would be in the region of eighty thousand Turkish pounds, or roughly fourteen thousand sterling. This was one of the few occasions on which the Istanbul station was required by Headquarters to justify expenditure for an enterprise in writing. The reply came by telegram, which was followed by an immediate initial draft for sixteen thousand Turkish pounds. This sufficed to start things.

The courier plane from Germany always arrived late on Friday afternoon and departed again early on the Saturday morning. We therefore always had to work pretty swiftly, if we wanted to give written replies to the questions asked of us. One day there arrived a packet about the size of a small box of cigars. It looked as if it probably contained official instructions, and as this was always an unwelcome part of the correspondence, I told my secretary to lock it up at once in the safe, or, if there was no room inside, to put it on top. When it was opened the next morning it was found to contain eighty thousand Turkish pounds in currency. Berlin had completely forgotten about the advance of sixteen thousand, so we now had ample funds with which to go ahead.

The first problem was how to get the money to Syria. One of our Arab friends suggested that we approach Ibn Saud's court administration. So far, we had had scarcely anything to do with this King of the Desert, and it seemed very unlikely that he would want to have anything to do with us. But he might, on the other hand, be ready to do a little bit of profitable business. The Germans, we suggested, should make payment to

19

him in Istanbul, and he should make the appropriate payments in Syria.

This idea, unfortunately, came to nothing, but the necessary arrangements were finally made through the wholesale food trade, which was for the most part in the hands of Syrians. The recipients in Syria were members of the highest families in the land, whose names are to this day to be found among the Ministers and similar leading personalities of the Syrian republic. They must, however, have been unduly incautious, for a number of them were arrested and the revolt fizzled out. Money was found to support the families of the notables who had been imprisoned, but even after a delay of three months there still appeared to be no prospect whatever of success, and eventually I was reluctantly compelled to abandon the entire project.

A not inconsiderable portion of the money had remained in the hands of the agents in Istanbul, and I felt constrained to require them to refund it. I was frequently told by my German friends that such a request was quite pointless, that I should never see a farthing of my money, and so on. To me, this seemed a test of whether I had placed my trust in the right people or not. One evening the head of the Arab group came to see me. From his waistcoat pocket he pulled out a little tissue-paper parcel; from various other pockets he produced another and yet another, until finally eight little packets were lying on my table. They all contained gold coins. Impulsively I told my friend Abdalla how delighted I was. He admitted that it had not been easy; his friends in the young Arab movement had told him that these were the only funds at the disposal of the younger elements, and they had urged him to invent some subterfuge in order to keep the money. But to this he had retorted: 'No! the Doctor has always been most considerate to us; we must be the same to him.'

Gold was readily obtainable in the free market in Istanbul; but one had to be very careful as to what sort of coinage one bought. There was the old Napoléon d'or, bearing the effigy of

Napoleon III with his imperial beard, but these French coins were not greatly valued. The highest price was commanded by the British sovereign, which in the market was called the King, on account of the King's effigy, but among the Arabs, who were much more interested in the charger of St. George on the reverse side, it was known as the 'Horse'. But even with British coinage one had to be cautious. Under the law of Islam, the reproduction of the human countenance is forbidden; in the case of gold coinage, the Moslems as a rule manage to overcome their religious scruples. But when such a coin bears the image of an unveiled woman, as in the case of Queen Victoria, this was too much for the strictly religious sects of the interior, and they refused absolutely to accept these indecent gold pieces; and so the Queen's sovereign could always be bought at a slight discount.

As the station expanded its activities, finance began to play an increasingly important role. Supreme Headquarters sent us a cashier who, unfortunately, was somewhat deaf. In the hot Turkish climate he had to work with his windows open, and since like most deaf people he was inclined to talk loudly, the cover-names of our agents and the amounts they were to receive boomed resonantly across the street for all to hear. Later we managed to exchange him for a more softly-spoken man.

On occasions, of course, we were in doubt as to whether some particular expenditure was worth while. On one occasion a relative of the Egyptian royal family told us that he proposed going on a business trip to Cairo in connection with his wife's property and that he would see political people of some importance. I discussed in detail the whole situation in the Near East with him, but felt that it would perhaps be a little tactless at this juncture to raise the question of finance. I therefore instructed one of my juniors to go into the matter of expense. Our friend's answer was that, in the first place, he would of course have to see the King, which meant that he would be expected to play tarock with him and lose. Then he would have to frequent the Mehmed Ali Club, which for his own purposes he would have no cause to do, and the club was a most expensive institution. All in all the expenses would amount to about ten thousand dollars and five thousand Turkish pounds, in other words some four or five thousand pounds sterling. It seemed to me that the military information would be well worth the five thousand Turkish pounds, but that the additional ten thousand dollars was a bit steep from a military point of view. I took the next train to Ankara and put the whole project before Herr von Papen, asking him whether the political aspect of the proposal was not worth ten thousand dollars to him. Papen replied that on those lines he was only too happy to do business with me and the problem was thus very satisfactorily solved.

The results were incorporated in five reports which were submitted for evaluation to Count Almassy, our acknowledged premier expert on Egyptian affairs. His comment was: 'I wish I could sign and claim these reports as my own.'

In one of the reports a statement by a Turk from Egypt was quoted. 'I have already once seen a nation in tears,' he said. 'It was when the leader of the Turkish people died; and now once again I am witnessing a nation in mourning.' The report went on: 'I refer to the consternation of the Egyptian people at the fundamental changes which have taken place in the King. Up to a year ago Farouk I was a really popular prince. He was not only personally respected and loved, but was also regarded as a worthy and stalwart fighter in the cause of the Egyptian nation. Since then he has completely changed both in his personal attitude and in his whole way of life. He appears to have broken completely with all the traditions of Islam and of his people. During the great fast of Ramadhan he was daily to be seen in bars and taverns; he went alone and did not wish to be greeted as King. He appears in all the clubs with his mistresses and frequently has too much to drink. The Queen, who is expecting a child, and the Queen Mother are taking advantage, in their own way, of the liberty which the King's philandering has granted them. The luxurious pretentiousness of the royal household with its six palaces in Cairo

22

alone, and the accumulation of fresh and ever greater scandals are the talk of the town, and have already led to an undermining of the royal authority, which will probably prove to be irremediable. The rest of the royal family, almost without exception, has quarrelled with the King; he refuses to accept any advice, political or personal, and anything in the nature of private and confidential conversations with other members of the family is avoided on principle. It is thought that, now that he has thrown in his lot completely with the British, the prospect of the collapse of the Axis and the consequent strengthening of his position, coupled with the lure of the Khalifate, which the British will grant him, have gone to the King's head. There are some who attribute his change of attitude to his youth; but the prime instigator, it is considered, is Nahas Pasha, to whose traditionally democratic and republican leanings many of the recent developments must be attributed. A further diminution of the royal authority and popularity, and with it indirectly of that of the whole royal family, will probably one day lead to an attack by the Wafd on the whole monarchical system and result in the creation of an Egyptian republic. Against such an attack even the heir to the throne, in spite of having managed to retain a certain measure of popularity, will be defenceless.'

This report was written in the autumn of 1943. But it was not until nearly a decade later that Farouk's fate overtook him.

In the same report the following opinion is expressed: 'Leading political circles in Egypt firmly believe in a total collapse of the Axis. They believe that Russia will emerge as the real victor of this war and that not only Germany, but also France, Spain, Italy and the Balkans will fall into her hands. They regard it as unlikely in the extreme that the Anglo-Americans will succeed in keeping the Russians out of the Balkans and Central Europe.'

In 1943, the receipt of reports of this nature was not welcome in Berlin. On principle, Abwehr stations were forbidden to take any part in political intelligence activities or to submit any reports of a political nature. But the somewhat unique character of the liaisons on which the activities of the Istanbul station were based made it inevitable that political reports should reach it in increasing numbers. And although it could be and was justified on the grounds that it offered opportunities for the opening of channels of military information, the maintenance of relations with Rashid Ali which the Ambassador had entrusted to me was in reality a chiefly political task.

It seemed a pity simply to pitch the mass of political information into the waste-paper basket, so I decided to pass it all on in private letters to the Ambassador in Ankara, with copies to the Abwehr in Berlin, in order that Admiral Canaris should be kept fully *au courant* with the political situation as it appeared to us in Istanbul.

From the Balkans, too, came plenty of political information. The gradual transfer of support by the Allies from Mihailovic to Tito was observed in good time. Of very practical interest were reports which cropped up from time to time of plans aiming at the foundation of a Balkan Union under Turkish leadership. In this, however, Turkish determination to act was lacking, for the Turkish Army still harboured, from the time of the Balkan war, a deep distrust of the Bulgarians. To-day it seems a little strange that this distrust should not have been dissipated by the fear that the Russians might seize control of the whole of the Balkans, as in fact they proceeded to do at the end of the war.

Among political questions the one great query was, of course, in which direction did the possibility of opening peace negotiations offer the most promise? By an American contact I was urged to try and stop Germany from insulting and abusing everything American. If only a friendly word was allowed to drop, I was told, such a gesture would certainly lead to the exploration of the possibilities of concluding peace. In his speech on Heroes' Day of Remembrance in February 1943 the Ambassador followed this advice, and his speech immediately resulted in a debate on peace moves in the American Senate.

In March 1943 the Turkish Foreign Ministry informed the Ambassador that the Archbishop of New York, Monsignor

1. German and Japanese intelligence officers at an inspection of Caucasian volunteers on the Russian front, 1942.

2. German and Japanese intelligence chiefs in conference with Subhas Chandra Bose (*seated centre*). Yamamoto, head of Japanese counter-espionage (*extreme left*) ; Lahousen (*second from right*) ; Nambiar, post-war Indian Minister in Berne (*extreme right*).

3.   Canaris (*extreme left*) travelling *incognito* in Spain, January 1943.

Spellman, was about to visit Turkey and had expressed a desire to have a word with the Ambassador or someone whom he trusted. The Ambassador proposed myself, but Ribbentrop intervened and prevented the meeting.

A third approach was passed on to me in April 1944 by my Turkish friends as coming from the American Naval Attaché and former American Minister to Austria and Bulgaria, Earle. As I was no longer in a position to deal with the matter, the task was undertaken on behalf of the Ambassador by Herr von Lersner.

Various other efforts of the same nature came to light—the Russian attempt to make contact, the efforts of the Japanese to arrange *pourparlers* with the Americans, and the continuous exchange of views between Russians and Japanese, who, of course, were not at war with each other until 1945.

The Japanese were most jealous lest the Germans should independently open negotiations with the Americans. My old connections in America, where I had lived for nearly a decade, were a thorn in their flesh, and on the demand of the Japanese Embassy in Turkey the Japanese Ambassador in Berlin, Oshima, complained about me to Hitler in March or April 1943. It is interesting to note that this *démarche* had no repercussions at all at that time; Hitler, obviously, had every interest in keeping open the door for negotiations with America, but unfortunately he was not capable of making proper use of his opportunities.

In February 1944 a member of my Istanbul Abwehr station deserted, with his wife, to the British. Regrettable though this undeniably was, it was a thing which might have happened in any intelligence service. But the wife of the man in question was a distant relation of the Ambassador, von Papen, and British propaganda inflated the importance of this young man to such proportions that the affair became a *cause célèbre*. Himmler, who had long wished to be rid of Canaris, made the most of this at Hitler's headquarters. Canaris was dismissed from his post, and I myself was recalled to Germany. In

C

August 1944 relations between Germany and Turkey were broken off, and the War Organization, Near and Middle East, came to an end.

Such, then, were some of my activities with the Abwehr. Many other men have, perhaps, more interesting or exciting tales to tell, but before going on to them I should like to describe what the Abwehr was, what functions it fulfilled and how it was organized to carry out those functions, and finally what use was made of it by the Supreme Armed Forces Headquarters which it served.

2

Espionage and Counter-Espionage

THE meagreness of the funds voted for the Intelligence and Counter-Espionage Services at the time of their creation in the days of the *Reichswehr*—the restricted armed forces allowed to Germany under the Versailles Treaty—compelled the Abwehr to see how and where the modest means at its disposal could be used to the best possible advantage and with the greatest prospect of success.

As regards long-range reconnaissance—this is to say naval and military espionage—in the West, little could be done at the moment; but the East offered a more promising field of action, and it was in this direction, with Poland as the focal point, that the Abwehr's efforts were initially concentrated. Later, when Hitler came to power, and the detailed conditions of the Versailles Treaty were ignored and the armed forces of the Reich expanded, the situation altered radically. The first task was then to conceal the expansion of the armed forces from the eyes of foreign intelligence services; meanwhile it was regarded as axiomatic that a Power aspiring to military parity with its neighbours must be furnished with precise information about the armies and navies of those neighbours. In 1933 the Chief of the Abwehr was the naval Captain Patzig; but as a result of conflict with the newly formed Gestapo and with other departments of the Third Reich, he was relieved of his post at the end of 1934 and was replaced by Captain Canaris, who, very shortly afterwards, was promoted Admiral. Much has been written about this remarkable man, some true, some less so. Since I knew him personally and worked for him, I shall conclude this book with a brief chapter about him. For he was more than the titular head of the Abwehr. His personality and

CENTRAL SECTION	FOREIGN SECTION
CHIEF: Col. (later Gen.) Oster	CHIEF: Capt. (later Adm.) Buerkner
DUTIES: All administrative duties on behalf of the other sections	DUTIES: Relations with foreign powers, in particular with allied foreign powers.
SUB-SECTIONS: ZF – Finance ZR – Legal ZKV – Administration and archives	

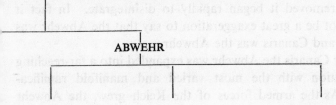

F: Captain (later Admiral) Canaris

ABWEHR

ABWEHR SECTION I	**ABWEHR SECTION II**	**ABWEHR SECTION III**
CHIEF: Col. (later Gen.) Piekenbrock	CHIEF: Col. (later Gen.) von Lahousen	CHIEF: Col. (later Gen.) von Bentivegni
DUTIES: Secret Intelligence Service	DUTIES: Sabotage and special duties	DUTIES: Security, counter-espionage and counter-sabotage

SECTION I

SUB-SECTIONS:

I H - Army
I M - Navy
I L - Air

GROUPS:

I Wi - Economics
I Ht - Army—technical
I TLw - Air—technical
I G - Photographs, Documents, Passports, etc.
I I - Wireless

SECTION II

SUB-SECTIONS:

II H - Army
II M - Navy
II L - Air

SECTION III

GROUPS:
III W (Armed Forces)

Sub-Sec. III H Army	Sub-Sec. III M Navy	Sub-Sec. III L Air

III C (Civilian security)

Sub-Sec. III C 1 Security in Government and official circles	Sub-Sec. III C 2 All other civilian security except industry and economics

III Wi: Industrial and economic security
III D: Transmission of false and misleading information to foreign intelligence services
III F: Penetration of foreign intelligence services
III G: Assessment and investigation, acts of sabotage, espionage, treason, etc.

(ADDED LATER IN WARTIME)
III KGF: Security in prisoner-of-war camps
III N: Security in technical communications depts.: posts, telegraph, wireless

methods moulded it. It was very largely his creation, and when he was removed it began rapidly to disintegrate. In fact it would not be a great exaggeration to say that the Abwehr was Canaris and Canaris was the Abwehr.

Under Canaris the Abwehr was expanded into a far-reaching organization with the most varied and manifold ramifications. As the armed forces of the Reich grew, the Abwehr assumed the name of the Department of Foreign Countries and Counter-Espionage at Supreme Armed Forces Headquarters (O.K.W.)—a department, that is, which was not incorporated in any one of the Services, but was designed to serve all three— Army, Navy and Air. As the attached chart shows, the department was finally organized as follows:

CENTRAL SECTION. Commander: Colonel (later General) Oster.
    Sub-Section Z F. Finance.
    Sub-Section Z R. Legal.
    Sub-Section Z K V. Administration and Archives.
The functions of this Central Section were purely administrative, on behalf of the other, operational Sections.
FOREIGN SECTION. Commander: Captain (later Vice-Admiral) Buerkner.
Duties: Relations with foreign powers and particularly with allied foreign powers.
ABWEHR SECTION I. Commander: Colonel (later Lt.-General) Piekenbrock.
Duties: Secret Intelligence Service, i.e., active espionage.
ABWEHR SECTION II. Commander: Colonel (later Maj.-General) von Lahousen.
Duties: Sabotage and special duties.
ABWEHR SECTION III. Commander: Lt.-Colonel (later Maj.-General) von Bentivegni.
Duties: Security, counter-espionage and counter-sabotage.

Each of these last three Sections was further sub-divided into three Sub-Sections, representing the Army, Navy and Air Force

30

respectively and numbered Sub-Section I - H (Army), I - M (Navy), I - L (Air), II - H, II - M, II - L and so on. In addition there were the following Groups:

Under Abwehr I

GROUP I - Wi (Wirtschaft). Economic and commercial information.

GROUP I - Ht (Heerestechnik). Collection of technical information for the Army.

GROUP I - TLw (Luftwaffentechnik). Collection of technical information for the Air Force.

GROUP I - G. Photography, secret inks, personal documents and passports, and all other appurtenances of a similar nature indispensable to the functioning of a secret intelligence service.

GROUP I - I. Wireless, including the design of wireless sets for agents and the organization of a wireless network for defensive and counter-espionage purposes.

Abwehr Section III—the Security and Counter-espionage Section—differed slightly in its organization from the other two Sections in that the three Sub-Sections III - H (Army), III - M (Navy) and III - L (Air) were not organized as independent sub-sections, but as sub-sections subordinated to a Group III -W (Wehrmacht—Armed Forces), which was responsible for the combating of espionage in all three Services. As some security organization was necessary on the civil side, a further group, Group III - C, was set up and divided into Sub-Groups III - C 1, and III - C 2. The former was concerned only with the surveillance and screening of government officials and employees, while the latter was responsible for the whole of the rest of the civilian field with the exception of industry, which came under the supervision of yet another group—Group III Wi. This last Group covered a very wide field, which included the activities of the Security Officers of the Armament Inspectorate and

Armament Commandos, who bore the title of AO.III.RU (Abwehr-Offizier III Ruestung).

Included in the combating of hostile intelligence services were the tasks of the misleading of foreign agents and the launching of true and false information destined by various routes to reach the ears of the opposition and to give him a false picture of the current situation. These activities came under Group III - D, and often—as in the case of the Sosnovski affair with Poland of which I shall have more to say later— achieved very important results.

Closely related to Group III - D were the activities of Abwehr Group III - F, to which was given the title of Counter-Espionage Group, but whose duties entailed not only the countering of the activities of hostile intelligence services, but also the penetration of those services and the planting of Abwehr agents within them.

Group III - G was the competent authority for assessing and investigating hostile acts of sabotage, espionage, etc ; it also undertook, on behalf of the military authorities, the task of advising on legal questions regarding treason.

Later, on the declaration of war, two further groups—Group III - KGF and Group III - N—were added, with the tasks respectively of preventing spying and sabotage in the prisoner-of-war camps and in the technical communications departments of the Posts, Telegraph and Wireless Services.

So much for the headquarters organization. The organization of the subordinate Intelligence stations attached to the various military district Commands and later to the Corps and Divisional Commands remained, in all essentials, as Admiral Canaris found them when he assumed office. With each military Command there was an *Abwehrstelle* (abbreviated designation 'AST.'), an Intelligence station under the direction of a so-called IC. A/O; IC., conforming to the abbreviation nomenclature in force in the General Staff, is that section of the staff which deals with the assessment, evaluation and collation of information received regarding the enemy, and A/O stands for

Abwehr-Offizier (Security Officer). These Intelligence stations were organized basically on the same lines as the Central Service; they were divided into Groups I, II and III, which dealt with collection of information, sabotage and special duties, and security and counter-espionage respectively. In addition they maintained advanced subsidiary stations at important strategic points, particularly in the vicinity of frontiers.

During the war the machine had to be expanded to meet the requirements arising out of the occupation of enemy territories, but the organization of both the Central Service and the various Intelligence stations remained essentially the same, with additions suitable to the local requirements.

From the very start of the Polish campaign Abwehr Section III organized Abwehr Commandos and platoons, to advance together with the front-line units in order to protect German troops from the activities of the enemy Intelligence service, to be on the spot to acquire any material which might be of Intelligence value and to seek out and capture enemy agents. This proved to be a useful and valuable innovation; it was repeated when the Western campaign began and achieved some outstanding successes. On the Western front Abwehr Section I also organized a front-line contingent which produced equally excellent results.

Bases in neutral countries must, obviously, be acquired in peacetime, if an intelligence service is to function in war. These bases were either camouflaged as commercial undertakings or were found some suitable niche in existing German official overseas Missions, and they were given the name of *Kriegsorganisationen*, KO. for short (War Organizations). War Organization Near and Middle East, of which I have written in Chapter One, was an example of this. When war broke out, Germany found herself cut off from many of her sources of information, and these KOs then acquired a very considerably enhanced significance.

Admiral Canaris regarded as one of his most important tasks

33

the solution of a problem which his predecessor had failed to solve, namely, the settlement of a firm line of demarcation between the activities of the Intelligence Services and those of the Gestapo and other Government and Party organizations. The Abwehr possessed no executive branch of its own; a military police force, such as is to be found in most other countries, had never existed in Germany in peacetime, and the Abwehr had consequently to rely on the co-operation of the normal police, and a harmonious working agreement had been reached with the so-called I.A. groups of the various police headquarters. This, however, had been upset by the advent of the Gestapo, which immediately claimed to be the sole guardian of the State and as Himmler and his chief collaborator, Heydrich, assumed control of one police organization after another throughout the whole of the Third Reich, the more insistent became this claim to a monopoly of security duties.

The Gestapo would in all conscience have had enough to do in assuring the internal political stability of the country. Not content with this, however, it became imbued with the ambition to set up an overseas political intelligence service—a type of organization which Germany had hitherto never possessed in any shape or form. In Great Britain the Intelligence Service is linked primarily with the Foreign Office and has always performed a species of mixed military and political services; but the political organization now set up overseas by the German Security Service, a National Socialist branch organization of the Gestapo called the *Sicherheitsdienst* or S.D., could not avoid overlapping with the Military Intelligence Service.

After much negotiation, an agreement was reached between the military Abwehr and the Gestapo, the broad lines of which were that the Abwehr should restrict its activities to purely military Intelligence, while the Gestapo agreed to refrain from any sort of military activity whatever and undertook to pass on to the appropriate Abwehr regional station, immediately and without comment, any military information which might fortuitously come its way, and at the same time to give the Abwehr

34

station full particulars as to the sources of the information concerned.

No political intelligence service, as such, was ever organized by the Abwehr; but as the line of demarcation is necessarily somewhat elastic, and as no purely military intelligence service can afford completely to ignore politico-military implications, a certain amount of political information was, of course, collected. Even so, these political reports were as a rule submitted chiefly to Admiral Canaris for his own personal information and for him to use as he saw fit.

The so-called counter-espionage—that is, the countering, penetration and misleading of hostile services—remained in the hands of the military Abwehr. All cases of counter-espionage in the field of activity allotted to the Gestapo had at once to be handed over to the appropriate Abwehr station; while in the circumstances it was unavoidable that the Abwehr should occasionally have to make use of individual branches of the Gestapo, the direction and control of the whole remained in the hands of the military. The relevant sections in charge were Group III F and Group III D. But since the Abwehr had no police force at its disposal, the operational aspects of counter-intelligence work remained wholly in the hands of the Gestapo, and whenever any police action was taken, a Gestapo official had to be present.

Further clauses in the agreement affirmed the determination of both departments to co-operate in the fullest and most loyal manner, and the complete agreement, which came to be known as 'the Ten Commandments', was at least the basis of a working *modus vivendi*. When difficulties arose, as naturally they not infrequently did, they were generally settled by appeal to the Ten Commandments.

Canaris realized clearly that the expansion of the Himmler-Heydrich organization would continue quite inexorably, and that the radical changes which would inevitably follow an outbreak of war would afford these two ample opportunity of extending the kingdom under their control. Grave friction would then become unavoidable. As a timely precaution, therefore, he persuaded the Supreme Command of the Armed Forces to make provision, in the event of any mobilization, for a Secret Field Police Force, which should come into being on mobilization and which would thus place an executive organ of their own in the hands of the Army and the Abwehr. The members envisaged for this force were for the most part selected from among the personnel of the Criminal Police, which so far had not markedly succumbed to the influence of the S.S., and from the lower ranks of the normal provincial police forces. In command was to be a Chief of Field Police, who would come under the direct orders of Army Headquarters, while the various units of the Secret Field Police would be subordinated to the various Army Groups, Armies and, in the case of occupied territories, military Field Commands in which they were serving.

Abwehr Section III, which was responsible for all active measures for combating the activities of hostile intelligence services, was subjected to severe tests each time any new campaign was being planned and prepared. It was the section's duty to censure, first, that the plans of the entral organization did not become known outside, and secondly, that such events as the movement of troops, munitions and stores, the significance of which might be deduced by observation of railway junctions, the contents of military trains, the direction of the flow of traffic and so on, should be shielded from hostile observation; if that were not possible, then Abwehr III must ensure that the information gained and the conclusions drawn could not be passed on to the enemy. Generally speaking, one solitary report on events of this kind does not furnish a sufficient basis for the forming of a correct and complete military appreciation of the situation; a clear picture can only be gained by the piecing together of a whole series of correlated reports. The archives of the French General Staff prove that the enemy intelligence services had gained neither timely nor accurate information regarding the preparations for the Danish and Norwegian campaigns, and Churchill himself in his memoirs states emphatically that the vast troop movements eastwards of the German Armies before the opening of the Russian campaign had escaped discovery by the British Intelligence Service. The concealment of these movements, then, must obviously have been most carefully planned and most meticulously carried out.

It was Abwehr Section III which exposed the participation of officers of the Air Ministry in the activities of the great Russian spy organization known as the 'Rote Kapelle', the breaking of which I describe in Chapter Seven. This, in itself, was no mean feat. The bonds of comradeship which link members of the Corps of Officers and the spirit of mutual confidence between superiors and the lower ranks which is a characteristic of the German armed forces rendered particularly difficult any unobtrusive observation of officers. Furthermore, Abwehr III had to act with great delicacy, since if this spirit of mutual confidence were in any way jeopardized or shaken by distrust, the whole inner strength of the German Corps of Officers would be destroyed.

The German Intelligence Service was highly decentralized, and a brief description of the organization and activities of a typical out-station follows logically on the picture just given of the Central Office.

'The principal field of activity of the Hamburg Abwehr station before the war was France and overseas. Until shortly before the outbreak of hostilities, its orders were to pay no particular attention to Britain; but at the beginning of 1939, as tension gradually increased, new directives from Berlin laid emphasis on the desirability of giving greater priority to the activities of intelligence work in England. As a general rule, the areas covered by each intelligence station were decided according to the geographical location of the station concerned; in the case of Hamburg, however, this principle was modified to a degree which enabled the Hanseatic port to take advantage of the exceptional opportunities which its world-wide connections offered from the intelligence point of view. Hamburg was given more or less a free hand to function in the Mediterranean, in the Iberian peninsula, in North Africa and in both the Americas.

Once the war had started it was of primary importance for the German Naval High Command to gain a clear picture both of the trade routes followed by shipping in South American waters and of the routing of the North American convoys, which— even before the entry of the United States into the war—were reinforcing and sustaining the campaigns in Europe and North Africa. With this object in view, a channel for the dispatch of written reports from certain South American ports was established by means of a mass of meticulously detailed work of the most varied and secret nature, including the system of communication by micro-point, the details of which have since been exposed. This last was one of the best and most ingenious systems developed by the German Intelligence Service, and one which baffled its opponents for a very long while. It consisted in reducing a page of typescript to the size of a full stop on an ordinary typewriter. By means of a specially designed punch, the real full stops were punched out from a perfectly innocent letter and the special full stops (i.e., the reduced pages of typescript) inserted in their place. With the help of a microscope the recipient could then enlarge and read the photographed page. Innumerable letters passed in this way through the enemy censorship without arousing the slightest suspicion, and the system was only exposed when an agent using it was captured and must have given the secret away in the course of interrogation. After that, the system, naturally, was regarded as compromised, since a censor on the *qui vive* could detect the inserted full stops by holding the letter to the light at a certain angle, when their presence would be betrayed by a faint shimmer.

'In South America a very considerable network was successfully established, which rendered quite excellent service for some time until it was penetrated by the Americans. Whether, as they were reported in the South American press to claim, the Americans discovered this network by methods of detection, or whether they only proceeded to mop up this network by working backwards, as it were, after they had acquired the secret of the micro-point system, has not been officially revealed.

'In this connection the following story is perhaps worthy of mention. A certain South American State concluded a treaty with the United States which was to be kept strictly secret, and an Abwehr agent succeeded in obtaining the text of it; his great difficulty, however, was to devise some means of transmitting his material to Germany. As it happened, a Roman Catholic priest was about to leave on a journey to Rome, via Spain, and he it was who unwittingly helped carry this exceptionally important document to its German destination. The agent succeeded in secreting a micro-photo of the treaty about the size of a postage stamp in the binding of the priest's breviary, and off he went on his journey to Rome. In Spain he halted for a while; there, in an unguarded moment, his breviary was snatched, the binding opened, the document removed and the breviary replaced on his bedside table. The micro-photo was then sent to Berlin, and the reverend gentleman was able to complete his pilgrimage, unaware that he had been an unwitting messenger of the German Intelligence Service.

'The document in question was of a purely political nature, and its evaluation was not therefore the concern of the military, but of the Foreign Office. Since Herr Ribbentrop had formed an appreciation of the political situation with which the treaty did not conform, he roundly declared that the thing was a fake, and so the whole painstaking effort had been made in vain.

'In connection with the Allied landings in North Africa early in November 1942, it is perhaps of interest to know that, among a whole number of similar reports, the Hamburg Intelligence station received as early as the beginning of October a fairly accurate one to the effect that an Allied landing in North Africa was imminent. In the last week of October came a further categorical report that the landing would take place in the immediate future, that the Allied forces involved constituted the greatest amphibious combined operation of all time, that the transports were then close to the West African coast under very strong naval escort, and that the objective was a series of landings at various points between Casablanca and Oran. The report was forwarded forthwith to Berlin, but as the source was not considered by the High Command to be of proved and absolute trustworthiness, the information was regarded as unreliable. This recalls to mind the old Clausewitz dictum about the Intelligence Service: "The most difficult task of a field Commander is to pick out the ones which are true from the mass of reports which reach him concerning the enemy."

'About the middle of July, 1944, some four weeks after the Normandy landing, my intelligence station received a report on the further operational intentions of the enemy from an agent who had proved himself to be a source of the utmost reliability. After clearing the Cotentin peninsula, the report stated, the British and Americans did not intend to make a direct thrust towards Paris, but to advance in a southerly direction towards Rennes and then with a wide turning movement to move on Paris from the south-west. The report was at once sent on to Abwehr headquarters, which in its turn passed it forthwith to the branch of the General Staff concerned. A few days later I received a telephone call from the General Staff Officer who was dealing with the report. He said that, as it gave no details of the number of divisions to be deployed in the operation, the report was valueless. To this I retorted that, while I considered it the task of the Abwehr station to obtain information as regards the enemy's operational intentions at the source of their inception, I was of the opinion that identification of formations to be used was the duty of the I/C. AOs (the Command Intelligence Officers) in the battle area concerned. Shortly after this passage of arms, the break-through at Avranches occurred, and the Allies' plan developed exactly as our agent had informed us that it would.

'A pre-requisite to the functioning of an intelligence service in Europe is, of course, the organization of adequate channels of communication. Apart from the use of the normal post, telegraph and telephone services, there are the secret channels which have to be built up piece by piece over a period of years. I do

Herzlichste Glückwünsche

zum Jahreswechsel

Raschid Ali El-Gailani

Herzliche Weihnachtsgrüsse
und
gute Wünsche zum Neuen Jahre

Amin El Husseini

OBERST FAUZI EL KAUKJI

BITTET

HERRN *Oberst d. G. Lahousen de Vivremont*

zu einem Teeempfang zu Ehren

seiner Exzellenz des

Grossmufti von Palästina

AM *Donnerstag* , DEM *11. Dezember 1941*

UM *17.00* UHR

IM HAUSE BERLIN NW 87, CUXHAVENERSTR. 18, II. LINKS.

---

4. *Above:* Greetings card from Raschid Ali el Gailani, the Iraqi Prime Minister.
   Centre: Greetings card from the Mufti of Jerusalem.
   Below: Lahousen's invitation card to a party given by Fauzi el Kaukji, the Arab
   leader, in Berlin in honour of the Mufti of Jerusalem.

5. A party given by Fauzi el Kaukji in Berlin on 11th December, 1941, in honour of the Mufti of Jerusalem. The Mufti is seated centre with Lahousen on his left.

not propose here to waste time on invisible inks and suchlike
primitive methods. The distances to be covered by these secret
channels are usually long, and the Military Intelligence Service
was therefore well advised, some time before war broke out, to
turn its particular attention to the transmission of messages by
wireless; in this again inventive genius, coupled with technical
Intelligence experience, played, of course, a decisive role. In
the schools for agents as much emphasis was laid on wireless
training as on training in the principal tasks of the acquisition
of military information. The Abwehr attached special importance both to the production of first-class wireless operators
and to the development of efficient and reliable wireless sets for
the use of agents. In time, our technicians succeeded in pro-
ducing wireless apparatus which combined a receiving set and
a transmitter in one small suitcase and which, in spite of their
comparatively small capacity of 20, 40, or 60 volts, developed
the energy requisite in time of war to bridge quite unbelievable
distances.

'To ensure reliable and efficient transmission of reports to
Germany the first essential was the installation of technically
first-class wireless stations at home. Apart from the one big
station at Headquarters in Berlin, whose primary function was
the maintenance of communication with the KO.s (the War
Organizations) and its own other subsidiary intelligence stations,
the remaining intelligence out-stations, such as Hamburg and
Vienna, whose lines of communications had to bridge great
distances, also required powerful and absolutely reliable installations. The Hamburg Intelligence Station, with little outside
help, had built for itself in one of the suburbs a wireless station
exclusively for communication between itself and its agents; its
receiving and transmitting sections were several kilometres apart,
the latter being directed by remote control from the former. The
receiving section was installed in the Europa-Saal and had some
twenty receiving sets and twenty-three further sets for overseas
communication. At these sets, the operators organized in
watches, worked to a precise timetable, listening for the reports

D

of their agents in Europe and all over the world. It was very important to pick up at the scheduled hour the first message transmitted by an agent newly sent overseas. The work of these operators was very nerve-racking, for often they had to wait in vain for days and even weeks for a sign over the air. If an operator succeeded in picking up an agent at the first time of asking—a feat which was extremely difficult to accomplish and one which demanded intense concentration—it was regarded as an outstanding success and was duly acknowledged as such.

'The transmitters were all governed by remote control and were installed, each in a separate concrete dugout, in a large open space. Approximately twenty transmitters could be connected to the receiving station by means of remote control and were also connected thereto by special telephones. Should the power fail, a large Diesel unit was in reserve capable of immediately rectifying the deficiency.

'The peculiar transmission characteristics of each trained operator were noted and recorded. Exactly as a graphologist can recognize a handwriting, or the expert can say with tolerable certainty who has written a certain letter on a certain typewriter, the 'handwriting' of each wireless operator is at once recognizable. Such recording was very necessary, for it enabled the instructor to check with reasonable certainty whether or not the sender at the other end was, in fact, the former pupil whose transmission he was awaiting.'

42

3

Propaganda, Sabotage, Foreign Relations and Evaluation

WE have seen that Abwehr Section I was responsible for active espionage and Abwehr Section III for counter measures against hostile intelligence services; as in all other countries, the armed forces of Germany felt the need of a further section for sabotage and special duties, and these tasks were allotted to Abwehr Section II, a brief history of whose inception and development is given below. The inclusion of these functions in the duties of the Abwehr Organization is one of the differences between the Abwehr and the British Intelligence Service, though the difference is perhaps more apparent than real. Such British units as the Special Air Service, the Long Range Desert Group and, on specific occasions, the Commandos worked as closely with the Army or R.A.F. intelligence organization as did the German Brandenburg Commandos with the Abwehr. Similarly all aspects of that military activity called 'psychological warfare' must be closely linked with intelligence activities in all armies.

During the first world war two new factors appeared which, because of the great part they had played in the collapse of the Central European powers, merited very serious consideration in German preparations for another war. The first was Propaganda, which contributed so much, in both Germany and Austria, to the undermining of the military virtues and the will to fight in the armed forces and to breaking the morale and resistance of the civil population; and the second, which applied particularly to Austria, was the appeal to national minorities and the inciting of dissatisfied and restive elements within the nation to co-operate in acts of sabotage.

43

Hitler, who came to power by means of agitation, fully recognized the importance of propaganda. He therefore created at Supreme Headquarters, for the common benefit of all three armed services, a Wehrmacht Propaganda Section and, with the deliberate intention of keeping it under his own immediate supervision, he attached it to the Operations Branch of the Headquarters Staff. The Section's main duties were the supplying of the troops with suitable literature, the compiling of the daily Wehrmacht Communiqué and the distribution abroad of information, news-sheets and pamphlets about the Wehrmacht. For the undermining of enemy morale the Section confined itself to the preparation of material, and the distribution of such material among the enemy was, to all intents and purposes, entrusted to Abwehr Section II.

Although these Sections only became active realities after the outbreak of war, the preliminary preparations were begun well in advance. It was the Sudeten crisis which gave initial impetus to these preparations. The Sudeten Germans formed a minority in the Czechoslovak State, and they were being badly treated by the Czechs. It was considered very desirable both to ensure the participation of these elements in Intelligence work and to make the necessary preparations for their active co-operation in the event of war. Among other ways in which they could be of use were the preparation of landing-grounds for air-borne operations behind the Czech defensive system—a type of military enterprise which was of course unknown in the first war—and the planning of acts of sabotage once war had started.

The idea of forming an 'Abwehr Platoon' for these purposes originated with Captain von Hippel of Abwehr Section II. An old colonial officer from East Africa, he was a man of great imagination and enterprise. At first he toyed with the idea of small groups of lost and desperate men surrounded by the enemy, the foe of every man and inspired to fanatical deeds by a burning idealism—or, in more sober terms, an isolated guerrilla force, devoid of either tactical or administrative liaisons. Initially he had no success either with the Abwehr or with Admiral Canaris, a violent anti-Bolshevik who sensed in the ideologies, which formed the bases of the plan, the seed of a bolshevist way of thought which he distrusted. It was only when plans for the Polish campaign were being made that a situation arose to which the Hippel idea seemed to be the answer.

The General Staff of the Army asked the Abwehr to take steps to prevent any destruction in the Polish-Upper Silesian industrial area, so that this district, which was of such great importance to the German war economy, could be swiftly incorporated without any loss of productivity into the German armament industry and programme. This, of course, was a typical Abwehr duty—the prevention of sabotage and destruction by the enemy. For the execution of their task the General Staff granted the Abwehr a few hours' liberty of action in Poland before the X-hour fixed for the invasion, 5.45 a.m. on September 1st, 1939. It was with some reluctance that the General Staff had agreed even to this brief period, for they feared that the secret of the beginning of operations might well be jeopardized by the Abwehr's activities; on the other hand, they were insistent that the invading troops must find no demolitions as they advanced.

To prevent the Poles from destroying important portions of their industry, such as factories and electric power houses, the Abwehr station Breslau formed a number of battle platoon with the title 'K-Trupps' (*Kampf-Trupps*), which were then incorporated into a unit called the Ebbinghaus Battle Group—a species of battalion of *francs tireurs* some hundreds strong, armed with small arms and hand grenades only. A certain number of these men crossed the frontier some days before the invasion, disguised as coal miners and workers, while the rest slipped across during the night of August 31/September 1. Before ever the military operations proper commenced they succeeded in occupying several important industrial installations, but once the initial surprise was over these lightly armed and unco-ordinated guerrilla bands were attacked by regular

45

Polish troops and gendarmes and found themselves hard pressed to hold out for the few hours before they were relieved by the advancing German units.

From this tentative operation two lessons were learnt. First, that a higher standard of training and leadership would be necessary for the future; and secondly, that these elements would, as then organized, become as it were unemployed after the first few hours of a campaign, and their enterprise and offensive spirit would thus be wasted from then on. Canaris therefore decided to adopt von Hippel's plan for the formation of proper Abwehr platoons. The most reliable and soldierly of Hippel's *francs-tireurs* were selected and invited to join the Wehrmacht as volunteers for special duties; thus they did not become either the secret agents or the adventurers that von Hippel had originally envisaged, but regular volunteers earmarked for special duty. From the very beginning Canaris was strongly opposed to anything in the nature of 'suicide squads', and he insisted that desperate enterprises offering little or no prospect of success were to be avoided.

On October 15th, 1939, the first of these units, a company with the designation 'Lehr und Bau Kompagnie zbV 800' (Special Duty Training and Construction Company No. 800) was raised in Brandenburg under the command of Captain von Hippel. By the beginning of 1940 the Company was transformed into a Battalion and placed under the command of a regular officer, Major Kewisch.

The successes achieved by the battalion during the Western campaign led to an increased interest both in the General Staff and at Supreme Headquarters in the further enlargement of these units. In October 1940 they were expanded into the Lehr Regiment Brandenburg (The Brandenburg Training Brigade), and in December 1942 into a Division.

The field of recruitment for these units was governed by the special nature of the tasks they were called upon to perform, and adaptability, imagination and, in some cases, a knowledge of languages were the principal qualifications required. These characteristics are particularly marked among Germans whose homes had been outside the boundaries of the Reich and many excellent recruits were found among the Sudeten Germans, the Balts, the Volga German colonists, the Swabians of the Banat, the South Tyrolese and, within Germany itself, among those who had returned home from Africa, South America and elsewhere. The process was cumulative, and those who first joined quickly attracted their friends and others with their own background. Subsequent replacements and draftings were undertaken by the Wehrmacht Overseas Volunteer Bureau, which was the organization dealing with all Germans from abroad.

Men were required who not only spoke fluently the language of their country of adoption, but who had also absorbed the habits and customs of the national majorities to a degree which made them for all practical purposes natives of the country in question. To put it more forcibly, if perhaps somewhat coarsely, they had to know how to spit like a Russian, if they were to be accepted as regular, dyed-in-the-wool *mujiks* by the Red soldiery. For not infrequently, indeed, did the success or failure of a whole enterprise depend on whether this grooming had been correctly and conscientiously or wrongly and superficially performed.

The recruits to the Brandenburg units also brought with them, among other things, genuine passports and identity papers from the countries in which they had been living, and these were most valuable to Abwehr Section I - G as patterns for the fabrication of false documents for agents.

To facilitate administrative, personnel and organizational routine, the Lehr Regiment Brandenburg (L.R.B.) was placed under the direct control of the Chief of Abwehr Section II—itself, of course, a formation of the Wehrmacht; apart from this, the troops themselves had nothing whatever to do with the Abwehr. Very often, however, in the preparatory stages of some enterprise, selected members of the Abwehr were attached for training to the Brandenburg Regiment, most of them being Germans or German nationals from abroad who were doing

47

their war work in this sphere of activity. Even so, the Command Staff of the Regiment, which on the orders of the Chief of Abwehr Section II led a very isolated and secluded life of its own, urged with increasing insistence that these 'Abwehr employees' should be kept right away from the strictly military articulation of their units As a result, the *Vertrauensmaenner Abteilung* (VM. Abt˙)—the Confidential Agents' Department— was formed, which was attached for administrative purposes to the L.R.B. but remained under the operational control of Abwehr II.

Later, in the middle of 1943, this VM. Abt. was expanded into a Brigade, with the title 'Das Regiment zbV 1000'. The essential distinction between the men of this Brigade and those of the Brandenburg Regiment was that the former were confidential agents in uniform; the planners of Abwehr Sections I and III could draw men from this unit for their enterprises, or they could send their confidential agents to it to do their requisite military service. But the Regiment zbV 1000 had nothing whatever to do with the Brandenburgers and their tasks.

When the Brandenburg Regiment was expanded into a Division in December 1942, it was placed under the immediate command of the Abwehr—that is, under Canaris himself. But this, too, was more or less a formality; tactically, the units of the Division, companies or battalions, came under the command of the Commander-in-Chief of the Army Group or Army in whose area they were serving. Training and organization were the sole responsibility of the brigade, and later the divisional, commander. All that Canaris did was to reserve the right to decide to which armies and in what strength Brandenburg units should be attached.

The permanent stations of the various battalions were selected according to the country of origin of the volunteers serving in them and the front on which they would most probably be used.

I Battalion (later 1st Regiment). Brandenburg. Earmarked primarily for operations on the Eastern front.

II Battalion (later 2nd Regiment). Dueren in the Rhineland, for the Western front.

III Battalion (later 3rd Regiment). Unter-Waltersdorf, near Vienna, for the South-eastern theatre of war.

Balts and German nationals from Poland were therefore sent for the most part to Brandenburg, and Swabians from the Banat and German nationals from the Balkans to Unter-Waltersdorf.

When the Regiment was reorganized in December 1942 on a divisional basis, it consisted of four Commando regiments— the 1st, 2nd, 3rd, and 4th Brandenburg Regiments—to which was added a fifth regiment, which later received the designation The Kurfuerst Regiment. The duty of these regiments was to provide officers and men for enterprises planned by Abwehr Section II. All regiments were reorganized and brought up to strength in Germany itself and were sent to the front in the spring of 1943. It was a tragedy to see how some of these troops, expressly trained for special duties and formed of the *élite* of the overseas Germans, had scarcely arrived at the front before they were grabbed by the local Command and swiftly frittered away in normal infantry combat.

For raids on enemy coasts and harbours a *Kuestenjaeger-Kompagnie* (Coast Ranger Company) was formed in 1943. Rommel, in whose Africa Corps units of the Brandenburg Regiment had served, was particularly interested in this Ranger Company; but owing to the entire absence of any support or assistance from the Navy, the Company never fulfilled the purposes for which it had been raised. Rommel attached great importance to sea-borne raids on the British coastal road and on lines of communication in Egypt, and it is of interest to note that he forbade the use of any sort of camouflage uniform, in spite of the fact that the British themselves had used a force of German Jews from Palestine, dressed in German uniform, for an operation near Tobruk—an operation which, incidentally, was a complete failure. Field-Marshal Alexander's nephew, too, was captured wearing German uniform but—contrary to

Hitler's 'Commando Order'—he was not shot, for Rommel had refused to pass the Commando Order on.

A word on the ruses of war, which formed the basis of the tactics employed by the Brandenburg units, would here not be out of place. The conception of a *ruse de guerre* is as old as the history of war itself. It runs like a thread through mythology and the story of the Trojan Horse is the classic example.

The employment of the Brandenburg units on the various fronts was based essentially on the *considered* and *organized* use of ruses of war, if possible in some novel form. In all these operations the primary objective was the achievement, through deception of the enemy, of surprise which could be tactically exploited by advancing regular troops, or could sometimes even be turned to strategic advantage by them. The combination of military objective and secret service methods gave these operations a peculiar character of their own, and their execution demanded of every man engaged in them moral and physical qualities of a high and exceptional order. In addition, these units were called upon to wage war in a manner which did not conform to the accepted rules of warfare, and for that reason membership of them could not be other than on a volunteer basis.

The Brandenburg units were lightly armed and equipped and were not suitable for long-range or protracted operations. While their specialized activities were originally confined primarily to the prevention of the destruction of bridges, means of communication, dams and similar objects of strategic importance, they were later extended to include every conceivable form of reconnaissance and shock operations, wholly or partly camouflaged. Long-range motorized reconnaissance platoons, for example, drove for many hundreds of miles behind the Russian front, and the stolid, close-cropped mujiks, lounging in Red Army lorries, were not for a moment suspected of being German soldiers. The Russian pay-books of the party had to be in order, the Field Post number of the letters in their pockets, allegedly written by their families from the Volga or the

Caucasus to their Nikolas or Vassili, had to correspond with the unit to which the soldier claimed to belong, and it had to be clearly and precisely laid down who was to feign sickness or deep sleep if the party was questioned. For not all the 'Russians' in these lorries could speak Russian; and some of them had only the dialects of Berlin or Hamburg. An enormous mass of meticulous technical work, carried out partly by the Abwehr Commandos attached to the intelligence section at Army Group Headquarters, but mostly within the Brandenburg Regiments themselves, preceded every operation they undertook.

Then, when the appropriate moment arrived, the decision had to be taken—'full' or 'partial' camouflage. In partial camouflage, only some articles of enemy equipment—steel helmets or overalls—would be used, to give the column an external façade which would allow it to approach its objective unchallenged. Immediately before the action started, these articles would be cast aside and fire would be opened. When full camouflage was used, when, that is, the whole unit was dressed in complete enemy uniform, the confusion caused among the enemy by the fire of their 'own' troops would be exploited for a surprise onslaught and the swift execution of the task.

In all such special operations based upon a *ruse de guerre* the primary essential was that the troops following up should arrive quickly enough on the scene to exploit the tactical and operational surprise achieved. This called for close tactical co-operation between the Brandenburg units and those regular units for whose benefit the *ruse de guerre* was being undertaken; not the least important part of this co-ordination was aimed at sparing the regular troops long and wearisome combat and heavy casualties—a consideration which contributed greatly to the understanding and appreciation which regular front-line units evinced for these novel special operations by the Brandenburgers. The average soldier had no very clear ideas about the activities of the Abwehr and was never in a position to see for himself the direct results of a secret service success; but for the operations of the Brandenburgers he had, as it were, a seat in the stalls, and every success of the Brandenburg Regiments brought tangible advantages to the troops which were obvious to all of them. These Brandenburgers were, understandably therefore, in persistent demand by Group and Army Headquarters Staffs; and when a unit was detailed, usually a company and sometimes, though rarely, a battalion, the commander-in-chief of the formation to which it was given assumed responsibility for deciding the form—full or partial camouflage—of its employment.

What is meant by the term sabotage?

Whenever anywhere in the world a disaster or an accident occurs, the cause of which is not immediately apparent, somebody is sure to cry: 'Sabotage!' In peacetime, when no special supervision by security services is exercised, this may sometimes well be the truth. In war, however, the perpetration of any considerable act of sabotage in the enemy country is among the most difficult of any of the tasks of a secret service. In Germany, in spite of the presence of millions of foreign workers, many of them working there under compulsion, there was no successful act of sabotage which could be rated higher than a completely insignificant pin-prick.

If a precise definition of sabotage is sought, then it is the putting out of action of some mechanism or organization by the secret dislocation of its functional activity, whereby the extent of the damage done and the period which must elapse before it can be repaired are of decisive significance. Only when these two are of considerable proportions can it be said that an act of sabotage has had any operational value in the military sense or has been really effective from the industrial point of view. Operationally effective, for example, would be the destruction of important lines of communication deep inside enemy territory; industrially effective would be the destruction of essential components of the armament industry, of important war research institutions, such as atomic energy laboratories, and sabotage against ships and aircraft. Subsidiary to these main targets is the very wide field of what is called minor sabotage, included in which is the effect of political propaganda, which must not be underrated.

Let it be said at once that the sabotage efforts both of the German Abwehr and of Germany's enemies achieved but very modest results. Only the sabotage attack by British and Norwegian Commandos on the Norsk-Hydro heavy-water installations in Ryukan in 1942, can claim to have been truly effective in the sense defined above. The reasons for this lack of success are primarily technical, and the chief reason is the great difficulty experienced in transporting the requisite amount of explosives secretly to the vicinity of the object to be destroyed.

For the study of the technical side of sabotage the Abwehr had at its disposal a laboratory in Berlin-Tegel, where a number of young explosive experts and chemists worked on the detonators and explosives which were to be issued to agents. Some of the benches of this laboratory looked more like the counters of a general store; at first sight they appeared to be laden with tins of provisions, thermos flasks, oil cans, suitcases, brushes and so on. But each of these ordinary articles had either a false bottom or a secret compartment in which explosives could be secreted. The detonators were for the most part either chemically or mechanically operated. Large numbers of the latter type—delayed action detonators of particular precision and design—were supplied by the Swiss; they produced, for example, a detonator approximately the size and shape of a cigarette lighter which could be set to explode after a delay of anything up to forty days and which could easily be secreted in the false bottom of a suitcase or some other such suitable place.

In November 1939, after the attempt on Hitler's life in the Munich Buergerbraeukeller, Himmler and his adjutant, von Alvensleben, paid a surprise visit to the Berlin-Tegel laboratory. Canaris attributed this visit to mistrust on their part. It was on this occasion that the leader of the S.S. made a quite fantastic and naïve suggestion to Canaris: he proposed that the

wine ration of the French troops be doctored with some substance not detectable by taste which would either stupefy or
act, perhaps, as a strong purgative, and would, for a time at
least, put the soldiers *hors de combat*! His particular interest was
aroused, however, when he was shown a special type of detonator for sabotage against aircraft, which was operated as the
result of the diminution in air pressure when the aircraft had
attained a certain height.

Sabotage against ships was exceptionally difficult. Most
attempts failed because of the impossibility of hiding a quantity
of explosives large enough to sink a good-sized freighter below
the water-line. Even when access to a vessel was feasible while
it was loading or unloading—always a difficult time during
which a particularly sharp watch is kept—it was almost invariably found to be quite impossible to place the requisite
amount of explosive in that portion of the ship, where its
explosion would be certain to cause sinking and total loss. The
number of ships, on both sides, which were destroyed through
acts of sabotage by agents, must be quite infinitesimal. But
regular under-water attacks, such as were carried out by British
Commandos and Italian divers in the Mediterranean, produced
very different results.

At sea also, therefore, activity was restricted merely to minor
sabotage, which now and again caused an inexplicable fire, a
curious mechanical breakdown or a mysterious explosion in the
upper works of a vessel. It was only on those rare occasions
when it was found possible to attach an easily smuggled
detonator to explosives which were already aboard that any
serious damage or even the total destruction of a vessel could
be anticipated with some confidence. On one occasion, for
example, a German agent who operated from La Linea succeeded in blowing up a British mine-sweeper, which was lying
in Gibraltar harbour laden with mines, by getting aboard and
placing detonators among her mine cargo. But such opportunities occurred very seldom.

Towards the end of the year 1939/40, Abwehr Section II

received instructions to try to dislocate Allied shipping in the Mediterranean and the Black Sea by means of sabotage. The bases from which these operations were to be conducted were Greek, Bulgarian and Rumanian ports, and, as it was desired to avoid any incident with these still neutral Balkan countries, the condition was imposed that all explosions must be arranged to occur when the ships were at sea and outside the three-mile limit.

Translated into operational sabotage terms, this task necessitated the use of precision delayed-action detonators as well as a most careful confirmation of how long the vessel would remain in harbour and exactly when she would sail. Even with this very general outline, it will be readily appreciated how greatly those 'unforeseen events' which constantly occur enhanced the difficulties of such sabotage attacks. On one occasion explosives were successfully secreted in barrels of fruit-juice, which were destined for a British freighter in a Greek port. The explosives were smuggled into position while the barrels were still in the hands of the Bulgarian purveyor. It then had to be found out or correctly forecast how long would be required for transportation by rail to the port, how long the ship would remain in harbour, on what date it would definitely be sailing, and how long the vessel would take to clear the three-mile limit, if Greek customs officials or other civilians were not to become the innocent victims of a premature explosion. In this particular case, the explosion did, in fact, occur on the high seas, great damage was caused to the ship's interior and upper works, but the vessel was not sunk. Many a promising enterprise had to be abandoned, however, because the three-mile limit condition could not with certainty be fulfilled and the consequent risk of serious political repercussions could not be accepted.

During the 1939/40 period there occurred one incident of a serio-comic nature. British merchantmen were frequent callers at Bulgarian ports, where, among other things, they picked up supplies for the French Levant Army in Syria, and it was decided to mix among the coal which they took aboard explosives prepared by the Berlin-Tegel laboratory to resemble lumps of coal which would explode when exposed to the fire of the boilers. One such British vessel came into Varna to replenish stocks, but found the coal to be of such poor quality that she refused to accept it and sailed away. Close on her heels arrived an Italian freighter which, to the horror of the Abwehr agents, leapt at the opportunity of buying coal at so cheap a price! The Abwehr had no choice but to come clean, tip the wink to their Bulgarian Security colleagues and at the last moment buy the contaminated coal back at an enhanced price. Only in this way was a ship belonging to an ally saved from having the boilers ripped out of her.

But whether it was coal, oranges or other merchandise which was doctored prior to loading on an enemy freighter, it was only on the rarest occasions and in the case of small and insignificant old tubs that the explosive charge was big enough to sink the ship. The Abwehr laboratory therefore set to work to devise some means which would enable special, remote-controlled torpedoes to be discharged from a motor- or rowing-boat at ships lying in harbour. The preliminary experiments were made on one of the Berlin lakes in 1942 or 1943. In technical theory the problem offered no difficulty; but the practical development of the idea came to naught, principally because the necessary co-operation of the Navy, with its very considerable experience and technical data on the subject of torpedoes, was not forthcoming. The bad relations between Canaris and Raeder, and the even worse relations between the former and Doenitz, who succeeded Raeder as naval commander-in-chief, certainly played a considerable part in this; the trade-union of the regular naval officers had little love for 'Canaris and his Abwehr gang'. The one exception was perhaps the Abwehr Observation Post in Algericas, which functioned—very successfully—entirely on behalf of the Navy as observers of Allied ship movements through the Straits of Gibraltar. For much the same reasons the experiments made in 1943 with frog-men and the attempts to set up a Coast Ranger Company within the framework of the Brandenburg Division attained no tangible result worth mentioning.

All the combatants found it practically impossible to launch any sabotage attack against hostile warships, either moored to the quayside or at anchor in harbour. Any such attempt was prevented by the exceptionally strict security measures taken by all warships when at rest in the proximity of the shore. When it is remembered what weight of explosive it requires in a torpedo to sink even a medium-sized cruiser, it will be appreciated that no agent working with a haversack, had any chance, of planting the requisite amount in the intestines of a ship. There remained, then, only sabotage against the machinery, which was, of course, possible, but which again was very difficult to carry out in such a way as to cause any lasting damage. A pre-requisite for this type of sabotage—not, of course, for attempts with explosives—is the co-operation of sympathetically minded agents in the ship's company itself.

Keitel's order to the Abwehr at the end of 1942 to prevent the sailing of the French fleet from Toulon by means of 'a massive sabotage enterprise' was, therefore, the nonsensical order of a layman. And, of course, it came to nothing.

The technical training of agents was undertaken at the Berlin-Tegel laboratory, but their instruction in sabotage tactics and the military training necessary for their employment as shock-troops at the front took place at Quenzgut, a small and well-equipped training camp situated in idyllic surroundings on the Quenzsee, a lake near Brandenburg. In addition to the modest barracks and the school buildings, there were also rifle ranges, wooden and iron bridges, networks of railway lines and other objects suitable for sabotage attacks. Instruction included the unobtrusive approach to the target, the silent overpowering of sentries by ju-jitsu, and finally the technically correct method of placing an explosive charge. A small laboratory, a lecture theatre and a gymnasium were attached to the main buildings, and the whole was completely hidden from the outside world.

The lake itself and a small fish-pond offered opportunities both for practical work and for recreation in winter as in summer, and a neighbouring aerodrome provided facilities for the demonstration and practice of parachute drops.

From about the end of 1942 or the beginning of 1943, every officer of Abwehr Section II had to undergo a course of instruction at Quenzgut, in order to get personal, first-hand experience of the capabilities and the limitations which would reasonably be expected of agents, and thus to obtain an insight into how to frame and allot tasks. When Indian, Arab or Ukrainian platoons came to Quenzgut to be trained for some special operation, then all but the small resident administrative and instructional staff disappeared.

In the theoretical lectures on sabotage the pupils were given formulæ of perfectly ordinary and innocuous materials which could be bought at any chemist's shop without arousing suspicion, but from compounds of which they could make up their explosives. Each student was then called upon to manufacture an explosive in this way and to demonstrate his ability to put together a home-made detonator. Having thus compounded his own completely home-made charge, he was required to carry out a practice demolition with it himself.

Taken as a whole, the school and training grounds on the Quenzsee provided all that was required for the instruction, in sabotage and in the use of the weapons appropriate to their duties, of the agents and personnel of a modern, up-to-date Secret Service.

Unlike Abwehr Section I—the purely active espionage section —Abwehr Section II was forbidden to engage in any activities, even of a preparatory nature in the United States of America until after the German declaration of war. Two considerations probably had considerable influence on the adoption of this decision. First, there was Ribbentrop's hope that he would be able to keep America out of the war, and his insistence, therefore, that any act of German sabotage which would certainly jeopardize the success of his endeavours be avoided at all costs;

and secondly, from experience in the first world war, we knew full well the tremendous propaganda storm which any German act of sabotage could arouse in the American press.

Abwehr II's only preparations for acts of sabotage in the event of war with the United States were confined, therefore, to its activities at the so-called 'Mexican base'. This base was supposed to maintain touch with an underground movement in the States, said to be of Irish composition, and with its assistance to plan sabotage attacks by means of explosives against shipping and armament factories. For the swift and secure transmission of reports the base was dependent on the wireless installation of the German Legation in Mexico, and this led to sharp friction with the Foreign Office and a demand from the latter that this Abwehr activity should cease at once. In the event, the whole affair proved to be a mare's nest and, from the Abwehr point of view, a most costly swindle.

When finally war was declared, Abwehr Section II had not one single agent or liaison man in the United States, by whom even any improvised act of sabotage could be contemplated. But Hitler, urged on by the Party executive, was demanding action in the States, and the Abwehr had no alternative but to try to ship agents from Germany to America. The operation was given the code-name 'Pastorius' and was most thoroughly and carefully prepared; indeed, a rehearsal of the whole thing was carried out under active service conditions, for the selected agents were ordered to carry out mock attacks on armament factories in the vicinity of Berlin, heads and secu.ity guards of which were not previously informed of what was afoot. In this hazardous exercise the Quenzgut-trained agents actually succeeded in placing their unprimed explosive charges in the very heart of these factories.

The U.S.A. squad was divided into two sections, which were put ashore from U-boats, the one on Long Island and the other in Florida. However, they were swiftly discovered and arrested.

To round off this picture of the organization of the Intelligence Service, some mention is necessary of the co-operation with the Services of allied and friendly powers.

Collaboration between the Abwehr and the Italian Intelligence Service (the S.I.M.) was already in active being before the conclusion of the 'Pact of Steel' on May 22nd, 1939. The Abwehr also had excellent relations with many prominent and pro-German members of the Italian Army, from whom it received timely information regarding both the statements made by Jansa, the Chief of the Austrian General Staff, to the Italian Prime Minister on Austro-German relations, and details of the defensive measures taken by Austria against the feared attack by Germany.

From 1937 onwards, Canaris was a frequent visitor to Italy, where he and Roatta, the Chief of the S.I.M. (a man said to be of Spanish origin) were wont to put their cards quite frankly on the table. Roatta was followed by the somewhat difficult Colonel Carboni, who had little love for the Germans and who, in his turn, was succeeded by the Piedmontese, General Ame. The blond and blue-eyed Ame, reserved by nature and sober and deliberate in his judgment, was in no way a typical Italian, and with him Canaris formed a close and intimate friendship.

An Abwehr KO. (War Organization) was set up in Rome, and the Italians sent a liaison officer to Abwehr headquarters in Berlin. The question of the South Tyrol was always a rather ticklish thorn in the flesh of Italo-German co-operation; immediately after the Anschluss, for example, the Abwehr felt compelled to accede to Italian wishes and withdraw from Innsbruck an officer who, originally a member of the Imperial Austrian Intelligence Service, had been the Intelligence officer in charge of the Italian Section. Then the Brandenburg Regiment, in which large numbers of South Tyrolese had been enlisted, was also the cause of a certain friction: the members of one of its units which was temporarily stationed in the North Tyrol had boasted in the local taverns that they would soon be home again in their own fatherland. These irresponsible words—grossly exaggerated—got back, via the Nazi Party organization in Italy, to Hitler, with the result that the posting of Brandenburg units to the North Tyrol was forbidden.

The Italian Intelligence Service had well-established liaisons in the Eastern Mediterranean, which, generally speaking, achieved good results, particularly in those ports in which the Levantine element preponderated. The Turks, on the other hand, who had no use for Italy and who harboured a grudge against her over the question of the Dodecanese, made life very difficult for the Italians. Hitler had left activity in the Arab world more or less entirely to his Italian partner, which did not in the least please Rashid Ali el Gailani, the Mufti of Jerusalem and several other Arab leaders. The Mufti was most skilful in the manner in which he played off German and Italian interests against each other; this aroused mistrust among the Italians, for whom any Arab movement was a source of anxiety, and who regarded any possible independence of the Arabs as a potential threat to their own colonial position in North Africa. For these reasons nothing came of the Mufti's suggestions for an Arab Centre in Libya, to stir up rebellion in Egypt behind the British lines and to support Rommel's operations. The Italians also refused to allow the Mufti to fly to Tunis, and insisted that he must be satisfied with a written correspondence with the Bey of Tunis.

Quite early the Italians made a special study of a field of activity, the significance of which was not realized in Germany until much later—the under-water sabotage attack. It was the Italian Navy which developed the technique that, towards the end of the war, became known as the 'human torpedo', or among the British as 'frog-men'. Dressed in india-rubber suits and equipped with fins and breathing apparatus, these human torpedoes were dropped in the vicinity of coast or harbour and swam under water to their objective—ship or harbour installation—which they then attacked with plastic adhesive mines. In the Normandy landings in 1944 the British used these methods to destroy the German under-water obstacles and clear lanes for the oncoming landing-craft. It was in 1943, in collaboration with their Italian colleagues, that the Abwehr Section II made its first experiments of this nature in the Olympic Stadium in Berlin. Further impetus was given to the idea by a meeting between the Chief of Group M, the naval group in Abwehr II, and the Commander of a Coastal Command in Kavalla. The results were reported, via Chief of Staff, Black Sea, to the German Admiralty, which immediately set about the formation of a Training Commando, entirely independent of the Abwehr, near Luebeck.

When the Allied troops landed in Sicily, the planned co-operation with the Italians in the so-called R-Organization (the Stay-Behind Organization) was put into actual practice. This consisted in the taking of all possible preparatory measures in those districts which might be voluntarily evacuated or inadvertently lost to the enemy; it included the leaving behind of agents with wireless equipment, the secreting of detonators and explosives for later use behind the enemy lines, and the placing of automatic, delayed-action bombs in barracks, administrative buildings and hotels which the enemy would almost certainly occupy. This was following the example set by the Russians. In 1941, in both Kiev and Odessa, a whole series of explosions occurred long after the capture of the two towns, which inflicted severe casualties, particularly among officers, in whose quarters and offices the bombs had for the most part been placed, and which gave rise to very considerable confusion. These bombs were not 'booby-traps', actuated by anything in the nature of trip-wires, but were delayed-action bombs, detonated mechanically or chemically.

Before the Anschluss, the German and Austrian Intelligence Services had a common interest in the reconnaissance of Czechoslovakia, in which country the Hungarians, too, were particularly interested. The Hungarian Service was the child of the old Imperial Austrian Service, whose traditions it maintained and whose skill it emulated. Canaris had fostered a very good understanding with the Chief of Bureau II of the Hungarian General Staff, and he also formed an intimate friendship with a young

General Staff officer, Szentpetery, whose photograph he kept on his office desk. During the first world war Canaris had served as a submarine officer in the Adriatic; it was natural, therefore, that he should find much in common with, and enjoy the confidence of, the Hungarian Regent, Admiral Horthy. Right up to 1941, when Hungary became a 'land-locked' island in the middle of the German domain, the results achieved by the Hungarian Service, which had its roots deeply and firmly spread throughout the Balkans, proved to be a most valuable complement to the information gathered by the active Intelligence Service of the Abwehr.

The Abwehr had a permanent liaison officer stationed in Budapest, and the exchange of information between Hungary and the Abwehr station Vienna, under Count Marogna, was particularly consistent and complete. This was due not only to the proximity of Vienna as compared to Berlin, but also to the fact that the Hungarians felt perfectly confident and at home in the Viennese atmosphere. The final act in this collaboration took place during the retreat through Austria, when officers of the Hungarian Section II were smuggled safely back to West Germany and were thus saved from capture by the Soviet forces.

Co-operation with the Japanese was based on an agreement to which Canaris had come with Oshima while the latter was still Military Attaché at the Japanese Embassy in Berlin. The Japanese Intelligence Service was highly organized in both the military and the political fields. At regular intervals its representatives, spread from Lisbon to Ankara, were called together in Berlin for conference. The Chief of this Military Attaché's organization was Oshima himself, and the Berlin Mission was composed of quite a considerable number of officers. Yet in spite of this theoretically excellent organization, a sharp split in the machine very obviously divided the army and the navy—a reflection of the almost unique situation which characterized the relations between army and navy in Japan itself.

In practice, the Germans were the donors in this co-operation and the Japanese were the recipients. Like busy bees they assiduously collected any and every sort of material and were particularly eager for technical information on such subjects as micro-photography, wireless, special detonators and so on. But whether they were ever able to sort out what was essential from the mass of material they collected and to make some corporate and coherent entity of it all is open to considerable doubt.

As they had not declared war on Russia, they should have been able to supply the Abwehr with intelligence from Russian sources which would have been of inestimable value. But in this respect they were most parsimonious; it was only where the Abwehr succeeded in suborning the sources at their disposal, and in the measure in which it was prepared to accept their evaluation of the material given by these sources that their neutrality was of any use from the Intelligence point of view.

On the other hand, the Germans had no control whatever over the extent to which the Japanese passed on information and material collected inside the German sphere of domination. To-day it seems pretty clear that, before the campaign against France, the Dutch and Belgian Missions in Germany worked in close collaboration with the Japanese Mission, and that from the latter they obtained initially the probable date, and later the definite date of the beginning of the Western offensive, although they appear to have made but little or no practical use of the information thus given them.

The relations between the Abwehr and friendly minorities in hostile, or potentially hostile, countries—one thinks of the Ukrainians, the Croats, Indian nationalists—were complex, but sometimes fruitful. An example of such an operation was the contacts between the Abwehr, and particularly Abwehr Section II, and the Flemish nationalist movement, which form a very delicate and intricate chapter in the history of the Abwehr Service.

The Flemish nationalist movement was made up of those inhabitants of Flanders who were opposed to the Walloon aspirations and who desired to see this Walloon preponderance swept aside. The Flemish nationalists were but a small minority in Parliament, but they played a very considerable part in the affairs of Flanders itself. They had nothing in common with those of their compatriots who were members of the great Belgian Catholic Party who had joined forces with the anti-socialist Walloons and who regarded themselves first and foremost as Belgians; the Flemish nationalist movement was prepared to recognize Belgian authority only if that country were willing to accede complete parity between Flemish and Walloons and to give effect to the political and cultural demands of the former. For them, the Belgian State was merely a diplomatically manufactured entity, to which in their consciences they felt they owed no allegiance; their loyalties were wholly to the Flemish race. They were unwilling to be drawn into a war against Germany to serve Franco-Walloon interests, and they supported with all the passion at their command the policy of neutrality preached by the King of the Belgians. They laid great store on good relations with Britain, and from the purely human and social viewpoint their sympathies leaned more strongly perhaps towards the British than towards the Germans. It was a great disillusionment for them when Britain finally came out on the side of the French conception.

They were not prepared in any circumstances to allow themselves to be robbed of their Flemish nationality—by the Germans or by anyone else. They therefore resisted with implacable will all the attempts made at Germanization by the S.S. In this the leaders of the Flemish nationalist movement, however much they may have disagreed on other matters, were completely in accord, and one of these leaders was flung into a German concentration camp as the result of the intransigence of his attitude. The S.S. seem to have been unable to grasp the fact that, although the Flemish were friendly disposed towards the Germans, they would resist to their last gasp any attempt to make Germans of them.

Nor did the S.S. appreciate that despite their quarrels with the established church, which they regarded as being pro-

Walloon, the Flemish were profoundly and reverently devoted to the Catholic faith.

Of significance from the Abwehr point of view was the fact that organizations of a Flemish nationalist flavour existed in the formations and units of the Belgian Army, through the medium of which the unity of that army could be disturbed and its fighting efficiency lowered.

The one major section of the Abwehr which I have not so far discussed was the Foreign Section, the *Abteilung Ausland*. This was not an essential or indispensable component of the Service from the organizational viewpoint, and the fact that it and the other three Sections of the Abwehr were all under the control of Admiral Canaris is attributable to the personality of the Admiral rather than to any real professional necessity. It was, indeed, not until the autumn of 1938 that the Foreign Section was incorporated into the Abwehr, and, in any case, a little later it was transformed into an independent department as is shown on the chart on pages 28-29. Until then it had been commanded by a colonel of the Army Headquarters Staff. This latter was relieved by a naval officer of equivalent rank by the name of Buerkner who had been in the Naval Intelligence Service and who retained command until the capitulation.

It was some considerable time before the tasks of the Section acquired precise definition. In brief, they may be summarized as follows. The Foreign Section was responsible for furnishing, to the three armed services, information of a politico-military character in the foreign press. It was also responsible for liaison between the Wehrmacht and the Foreign Office and for the study of foreign political affairs in so far as these affected the Wehrmacht.

These duties frequently over-lapped with the activities of the armed services; but thanks to the cordial co-operation which existed, there was practically no friction of a serious nature.

The final decision on all great problems in the foreign

political field were taken by Hitler himself, in person. There was, however, a further and subsidiary field which merited full attention, for in time of war all foreign political problems, big and little, have some military significance. During the second world war the Section worked on a comparatively independent basis, and the only thing which interfered somewhat with its work was the almost pathological anxiety of Ribbentrop lest anyone should meddle in foreign affairs and rob him of something which he regarded as his own prerogative and his alone. This attitude of the Foreign Minister was counterbalanced, however, by the fact that the vast majority of the Foreign Office officials from the Secretary of State downwards were both accessible and eminently reasonable.

The Foreign Section was also the link between Supreme Headquarters of the Wehrmacht and the Attachés, both German Attachés abroad and those of foreign powers accredited to Berlin, of the three armed services—Army, Navy and Air. Before agreeing between the wars to the re-introduction of Service Attachés with the German diplomatic missions abroad, the Foreign Office, as a result of its experiences primarily with the Military Plenipotentiaries of Kaiser Wilhelm II in 1914/18, had made it a condition that none of these Attachés should have anything to do with the Secret Intelligence Service, should employ no agents of any sort and should always submit his reports before dispatch for counter-signature by the head of the mission to which he was attached.

The three services had been at pains to select efficient and experienced officers for the posts of Attachés to foreign capitals, and while the rules of the game imposed by the Foreign Office were obeyed, a healthy stream of usually excellent reports flowed in to the headquarters of the respective services, and to Supreme Headquarters of the Wehrmacht via the Abwehr Foreign Section.

It was, however, doubly unfortunate that quite a number of these first-class reports were never submitted to Hitler himself, with whom the final decision lay, and that many of the conclusions drawn in the reports that did reach him were rejected by him, if they failed to conform to his own ideas on policies. Apart from the information received from German Attachés, the liaison between the Abwehr Foreign Section and the foreign Attachés added many pieces to the mosaic of the politico-military situation which was always in process of gradual creation for the benefit of the Wehrmacht; the picture was carried a step further towards completion by the information gathered by the sources reporting to the other Abwehr Sections; finally, the quite exceptionally cordial relations established by Admiral Canaris with the Secretary of State in the Foreign Office, the heads of the German diplomatic missions abroad, the foreign diplomats in Berlin, the heads of States and other important personalities in allied and neutral countries were of immense value and importance. As *ultima ratio* the Admiral was always at hand in the background to throw his weight into the scales if the Foreign Section could not come to an agreement with the Foreign Office or with some other department more influential than itself. In this way, and quite apart from the activities of the Foreign Office and the innumerable other government departments which intervened in foreign affairs, there emerged a pattern of changing and ever-growing design, from which much valuable information could be culled; and to keep the Service Attachés overseas abreast of the knowledge possessed at home, a regular précis of information received was prepared and periodically dispatched to them through the headquarters of their respective services. So strict were the rules governing secrecy and security, that this was a somewhat Sisyphus-like task; even so, and in spite of many disappointments, the Foreign Section did succeed in keeping the overseas officers *au courant* with current affairs.

In the same manner, formations at the front, down to divisions, were furnished with a monthly review of the foreign political situation; and the Foreign Section was encouraged in its determination to maintain these two periodical reviews by the knowledge that other German organizations abroad were also most anxious to receive copies, as they were very seldom sent anything of the kind by their parent department at home.

The Foreign Section was also the competent authority on international law, in so far as it was concerned with military matters. With the collaboration of such outstanding men as Professor Schmitz of Berlin University and Hellmuth, Count Moltke Kreisau, the Section consistently and uncompromisingly strove for the strict observance of international law. For example, it adopted a very firm attitude on the subject of Hitler's orders for the treatment of Russian prisoners-of-war, which it categorically condemned as a purposeless contravention of such law. This attitude was further strongly supported by Admiral Canaris, himself a confirmed believer in the sanctity of international law; but though it may have been the cause of some improvement, its final influence on the highest circles remains doubtful.

Under the Foreign Section was a further sub-section charged with the maintenance and supply of auxiliary cruisers and blockade runners overseas. In reality this was a purely naval occasion; but the sub-section had originally been formed by Admiral Canaris, and he was unwilling to relinquish control of it in war, although he had but little time to devote to it. It was, however, one of his favourite progeny, and its quite astonishing successes were far greater than could ever have been expected of it.

Finally, before turning to the Abwehr in operation, it is necessary to say something about the way the information collected was evaluated and used. Here we come up against the greatest weakness of the whole German intelligence system, but one for which the Abwehr was not itself in any way responsible. This weakness resulted from the organization of the Supreme Command of the armed forces, and therefore I fear that it is essential here to give a brief description of what that organization was.

In theory it was excellent, and was based on the lessons of

experience learned in the first world war. The head of the State was the supreme commander of the armed forces. Under him was a commander-in-chief armed forces, a military man with his own headquarters (*Oberkommando der Wehrmacht*): with this headquarters, which theoretically dealt only with plans and decisions on the very highest level, was the *Wehrmachtfuehrungsstab* (Armed Forces Command Staff), and, among other staff organizations, the headquarters of the Abwehr (since the Abwehr, as has been already stated, served all three services). The next echelon consisted of the headquarters of the Army (*Oberkommando des Heeres*), of the Navy, and of the Air Force, each with its own commander-in-chief. In theory, as I say, it was an excellent system. In practice it was not so, for a number of reasons.

First of all Hitler, once he had got rid of Blomberg in 1938, assumed the position of Commander-in-Chief Armed Forces in addition to his rightful prerogatives as Supreme Commander. This meant that a civilian had the last say in matters which were of a military nature. However, so celestial, in theory, were the fields in which the O.K.W. was supposed to function, that this, in wartime at least, was not necessarily harmful. But that was not the end of his encroachments. After the departure of Field Marshal von Brauchitsch in 1942 Hitler appointed himself Commander-in-Chief of the Army too. Here he was far more involved in day-to-day matters of which he knew little and where he could, and did, do considerable damage to the German military effort.

Furthermore, the Supreme Headquarters, the O.K.W., was soon made to function in a role for which it had not been designed. While Army headquarters, the O.K.H., was responsible for the war on the Russian front, Armed Forces headquarters was made responsible for the control of operations on all the other fronts. The result was that we had two supreme staffs, both commanded by the same civilian, fighting two independent and separate world wars. The remarkable thing is that this ramshackle and illogical system functioned as well as it did, and for this the devotion to duty and intelligence of the General Staff officers at both headquarters is primarily responsible. Meanwhile, however, another result was that the primary task of the Armed Forces Command Staff—the planning and control of the operations of the armed forces as a whole and the direction of Germany's war effort at the highest level— gradually became well nigh impossible.

There were other weaknesses, for which personal relations were largely responsible. Goering, as Commander-in-Chief of the Luftwaffe, was also the second man in Germany. As such he was not particularly anxious to accept directives which displeased him from the O.K.W. Himmler, as Commander-in-Chief of the Armed S.S., the Nazi private army which was continually expanded until by the end of the war it numbered some twenty divisions, behaved in similar fashion. This weakening of the authority of the O.K.W. affected the Abwehr indirectly only.

What did affect it directly was that any thorough evaluation by the General Staff, Supreme Headquarters Armed Forces, of the mass of intelligence material placed before it by the Abwehr soon became quite out of the question. Not only did the other pressing military tasks of the O.K.W. of the most vital and urgent nature—the executive command, that is, of all fronts except the Eastern theatre—allow very little time for such evaluation; but also there was no special branch of the O.K.W. detailed exclusively to deal with this militarily extremely important duty.

In fact it was the headquarters staffs of the three services which evaluated the information collected by the Abwehr. This meant that while Abwehr headquarters was, as it had to be, with the O.K.W., it was serving directly the O.K.H., the O.K.L. and the O.K.M. The Supreme Headquarters of the Army would thus receive information which had been neither evaluated nor sifted as it should have been at a higher level. Such information would be passed, still in its rougher form, to one of its two intelligence offices, Foreign Armies West or Foreign Armies

East. Such an office was led by a staff officer, probably a brilliant one, but by the middle of the war he might well be a young colonel in his mid-thirties whose previous appointment had been chief of staff of an army corps and whose knowledge of military intelligence, although adequate for front line operations, was nil so far as the somewhat esoteric matters of the Abwehr were concerned.

It was, in fact, a most unsatisfactory system. And there lies the explanation for the failure to evaluate correctly reports about the Allied landings in North Africa and about Allied plans in Normandy. Such incidents as these were not of rare occurrence, either. Indeed, when one considers the chaos that existed in the organization of the Armed Forces at the highest level, it speaks volumes for the devotion and efficiency of Abwehr officers and General Staff officers alike, that German Intelligence functioned as well as it did.

As for the further confusion caused by the jealousy of Ribbentrop, with his private intelligence service, and Himmler, with his Security Service, I have referred to this before and I shall have occasion to speak of it again.

4

Poland, Denmark, Norway

IT will be recalled that during the Weimar period the Abwehr was a very small organization, divided into two sub-sections, Sub-Section West and Sub-Section East. In view of the very limited facilities and funds available, it had no choice but to concentrate on questions of the most immediate and direct importance. There could be no hope of building up a mass of information about countries remote from Germany, or of planting networks of agents against very distant, possible contingencies. The two sub-sections therefore devoted their attentions to Germany's immediate neighbours and most probable enemies in the event of any future war.

The focal point of Sub-Section East's principal activities throughout the 'twenties and 'thirties was Poland, in which country the Abwehr undertook the dual task of countering the activities of the Polish Intelligence Service and of obtaining information about the newly formed and rapidly expanding Polish Army. Against Soviet Russia no systematic intelligence system was organized at this time; German activity here confined itself to making the most of such chances as fortuitously came its way. Up to the beginning of the 1930s it was indeed occasionally found possible to send individual spies and confidential agents into Russia, but the Polish frontier was always much easier to cross.

It was stated that the Polish Army was to be brought up to a strength of sixty divisions, and the German Intelligence Service did its best to keep abreast of this intensive programme. The task fell into two parts. The first part consisted of the organization of a so-called 'covering network', a spiderweb of confidential agents spread across the land to observe every point of

73

importance, which included not only centres of direct military importance but also such technically vital installations as the railways and so on. These agents remained quiescent, with orders to report only when anything of military or politico-military importance occurred, when they were expected to go automatically into action, without waiting for any specific instructions from their superiors. Most of these confidential agents worked on a voluntary basis. The many periods of tension and crisis to the east of Germany during the years 1921–30 gave the machine ample opportunity to run itself in, and the results it ultimately obtained were very satisfactory.

The second part of the task was the collection of information about the Polish Army and its entire organization. To a certain extent this was achieved by such painstaking and laborious routine work as the meticulous study of the Polish daily press and other generally available publications; reports on social events, accidents, the births and deaths columns, accounts of new constructional works and other advertisements afforded numerous indications both of the normal Order of Battle and of any particular troop movements. After a while, however, it became apparent that the Polish press, and particularly the principal newspapers, were being well directed from the security point of view, and as time went on the volume of information available from such sources diminished steadily.

In addition, direct sources of intelligence had to be established, and this necessitated the finding of Polish officers, and of government officials concerned with national defence, who were willing to pass on information. Only through these channels was it possible to obtain details of such militarily important documents as mobilization schemes, descriptions of weapons and armaments, military operational plans and so on. Such agents were to be found primarily among individuals in urgent need of money, but the reverse side of the picture is, of course, that this type of person is normally very free with his money when he has any, and that his sudden somewhat lavish expenditure usually attracts undesirable attention—a common enough story in all countries throughout the ages. Subsequent courts martial on charges of espionage led to much stricter screening of Polish officers and to a tightening up of routine security measures, which, up till then, had been somewhat neglected. The most secret documents, for instance, had originally been kept in ordinary metal dispatch boxes, very easy to open, and it was only later that the use of burglar-proof safes and steel cabinets was gradually adopted.

It is certainly of interest to note that, apart from the officers, non-commissioned officers and government employees who worked for money, quite a large number of senior and important people, who certainly had no financial need to do so, voluntarily offered their services; and all experience since the inception of the German Intelligence Service in 1866 has taught that the most valuable and efficient agents are precisely those who do volunteer.

The Tolodzietzki case affords a good example. The most important of all the Polish Intelligence bureaux was situated in Bromberg, under the command of Captain (later Major) Zychon, one of the ablest and most fertile-minded officers in the Polish Service, who was also in charge of eleven subsidiary Intelligence posts. In Danzig was the General Commissariat of the Polish Republic, and it was, of course, easy for the Poles to install an intelligence section within the framework of this body; this section was also under Zychon, who used to visit Danzig frequently. While there he had the habit of ringing up his German opposite numbers and chatting with them in a most amiable way, though sometimes—dependent upon his degree of intoxication—he would curse them roundly in the most uncouth fashion.

Suddenly, in 1930, a Polish officer named Tolodzietzki voluntarily got in touch with one of the intelligence stations of the Eastern Sub-Section. He was working under Zychon in the Bromberg bureau and offered to tell all he knew about that organization. The German station immediately came to the conclusion that the whole affair was a plant and refused to have anything to do with the man. A little later, however, Tolodzietzki was arrested by the Poles and hanged out of hand, and it was only after his death that it was found out that the material which he had offered was not only absolutely genuine but also of the utmost importance.

Of considerable interest, too, is the story of the man to whom the German Intelligence Service was indebted for the best report on Polish preparations for an offensive. He was a master in the art of recruitment for the Intelligence Service, and, with a quite exceptional gift for handling men, he succeeded in enlisting the services of quite a number of senior officers holding important command posts. He also was a volunteer, and he also was initially rejected by the Germans. Unlike Tolodzietzki, however, he was successful in keeping his attempted liaison with the Germans secret from the Poles and so continued in his appointment. When the disappointed Germans realized what first-class material he had offered them, they did their utmost to regain touch with him, but two and a half years passed before they were able to arrange a further meeting. In time, however, he too fell under suspicion of working for the Germans, and the latter were most anxious for him to remain in Germany, where he would be safe. But he turned a deaf ear to all their urgent representations; driven by the strength of his attachment to the woman he loved, he returned to Poland, where he was promptly arrested.

When the Polish campaign opened, he, with hundreds of other prisoners, was transferred eastwards on foot. As soon as he and his companions got wind of the presence of the German armoured vanguards in the vicinity of Brest Litovsk, they broke away and escaped. An agent established contact with the leading German troops and succeeded in obtaining an interview with their commander, who believed his story and sent him on, within a day or two, to the appropriate German Intelligence station. Later he was used by the Germans for Intelligence work against Soviet Russia, and here, too, he rendered excellent service. When the campaign against Russia started he was seconded to a front-line reconnaissance unit, in which he was invaluable as an instructor of agents. Finally, however, he was ambushed by one of his own agents and shot.

In these intelligence activities it was of great importance to be able to make use of the work done by the German Criminal and Frontier Police Forces, which were not, however, subordinated to the Army but to the Prussian Ministry of the Interior. At first the collaboration promised to develop along satisfactory lines; but then there occurred an incident which put an abrupt end to all further co-operation. The Polish Intelligence Service was anxious to get hold of the latest pattern German gas-mask; however, instead of doing this through their Section II, which would have been the appropriate branch, it ordered the so-called Frontier Guard to obtain one. One of the Poles approached a German N.C.O., who listened to what he had to say and then reported the matter to his superiors; then, in accordance with orders, he wrote a letter to the Pole which the latter accepted in such good faith that after a number of further meetings he agreed to cross the Vistula with a colleague and meet the German N.C.O. in a small hut which was used as a passport inspection office. As the gas-mask was being handed over, hidden Germans sprang out, and a shooting affray ensued, in which one of the Polish Commissars received a mortal wound from which he later died. The second Commissar was sentenced to fifteen years' penal servitude, but was subsequently exchanged. This incident, which figured quite prominently in the foreign press, so shook the equanimity of the Ministry for the Interior that all collaboration stopped for a very long time to come.

Meanwhile the Polish Intelligence Service in Germany itself was by no means inactive. Many experts maintain that the Poles, in the realms of intelligence work, are the most gifted people in the world, and what the Polish Intelligence Service had accomplished became clear to the Germans when Warsaw was taken and the greater portion of the Polish Intelligence archives fell into German hands. The Polish Section II had its offices in the Pilsudskego Square, but when they were seized on October 1st, 1939, there was not a file in the place. There were over a hundred locked safes which were gradually opened by experts and which all proved to be practically empty. On the whole, the haul was a poor one; though in the sub-section which had dealt with Germany quite a mass of interesting material was found, among other things a very complete and detailed printed handbook of the German Wehrmacht, with, in some instances, the name of the German source who had furnished the information. Further, there were some excellent military maps, the directories and telephone directories published by the German postal services and most voluminous card indices referring to Soviet Russia and to emigrants all over the world. But of particulars of any German agents working for the Poles there was not a sign.

A little later, however, a German officer going one day for a stroll past one of the old forts—Fort Legionov, a relic of the Czarist epoch, now devoid of any importance as a military installation—observed that the door was ajar and went in. He found himself in a species of a strong-room, filled with filing cabinets and a great number of bulky packages. On examination they were found to contain not only the complete files of the reports from the Polish Military Attachés in Tokio, Rome and Paris, but also a mass of incriminating and gravely compromising material from the Bromberg and other Intelligence Bureaux, which led to a whole series of courts martial.

Then there was the case of Mademoiselle Shebinska. This lady lived in Danzig and had succeeded in striking up a friendship with a gentleman of the German Abwehr, from whom in the course of normal social intercourse she managed to extract odd bits of information about his official activities. The Germans had not infrequently been surprised at the way in which timely Polish counter-measures had interfered with some plan in hand, and they had suspected treachery; it was only after this mass of files was found that it was learned that Mademoiselle Shebinska, after first being subjected to pressure by Major Zychon, had been enlisted by him and worked for the Poles for a long time.

A great deal of light was also thrown by this find on the case which may well be regarded as the climax of the struggle between the German and Polish Intelligence Services—the Sosnovski affair, which occurred in 1935, the first year in office of the new Abwehr chief, Captain Canaris. Sosnovski, a good-looking man, elegant in appearance and polished and suave in manner, first appeared in Berlin in 1927, where he set up house in a most lavish style and claimed to be the representative of a 'Supra-national Committee for the Combating of Bolshevism'. He very quickly gained the *entrée* into Berlin society, entertaining regally and spending, on his own admission, more than a million marks a year—a sum which exceeded the whole annual expenditure of the Abwehr Service of that time. With a certain *divorcée*, Frau von Falkenhayn, he formed a liaison which, on the lady's side, blossomed without any doubt into deep and sincere love. A letter she wrote shortly before her death was conclusive proof of the effect he had had upon her. For Sosnovski, however, she was merely a tool for the furtherance of his espionage activities. With her assistance he made friends with two women working in the German Ministry of Defence. They became frequent visitors to his house, and succumbing to the charm of his personality, allowed themselves to be persuaded to give him copies of important documents relating to Germany's plans of operation against Poland.

Apart from the amorous liaisons which were of use to him in his capacity as an intelligence officer, he also formed an attachment with Lea Niako, a ballet dancer of the German Opera House; and here he met with more than his match. In a moment of weakness he let drop hints about his real activities; through the intermediary of a highly placed friend, Lea Niako passed on this information to the Abwehr, and then the struggle between the Intelligence Services was joined. Piece by little piece the whole mosaic gradually took shape, until at last the moment for action arrived. The Abwehr struck, and Sosnovski was arrested—at one of his own parties.

The case against all the accused was heard in the People's Court. In the difficult situation in which he found himself Sosnovski was most skilful in his own defence and most considerate to those accused with him. But Frau von Falkenhayn and one of the women of the Ministry of Defence were sentenced to death, while the other woman was condemned to fifteen years' penal servitude and Sosnovski received a life term. Of it, however, he served but little. The Polish Government opened negotiations, as a result of which he was exchanged for four German agents—one of them a woman—who had been arrested in Poland.

About the time of Sosnovski's return to Poland, the Polish General Staff had received a German plan of invasion which had been suitably doctored by the Abwehr and played into their hands. The Poles believed that this bogus plan was genuine and that the plan brought to them by Sosnovski—which was, in fact, genuine—was a forgery, compounded with his knowledge and assistance. As a result the unfortunate Sosnovski was sentenced to twelve years' penal servitude by the Poles, and Germany emerged from the whole affair unscathed.

When Poland was invaded in 1939 Admiral Canaris instituted a search for Sosnovski. After long and painstaking inquiries it was ascertained that when the Polish prisons were thrown open such prisoners as were serving a sentence on account of treason had been shot. After the war there were rumours that Sosnovski had, after all, escaped and had gone back to his old activities.

The frustration of Polish attempts to penetrate German military units was a source of constant anxiety and trouble. Lack of personnel in the Abwehr stations precluded the possibility of giving intensive or even adequate instruction to the troops—both officers and men—on the attitude to be adopted towards attempted enemy espionage. It can, however, be said that, with the exception of one case of grave dereliction of duty, nothing untoward occurred. As a general rule the German soldier, approached with an offer to serve an eastern intelligence service, invariably reported the matter to his superior officer.

The one exception was the case of a very gifted non-commissioned officer who voluntarily entered the Polish Intelligence Service. When on the point of exposure he succeeded in fleeing to Poland whence he managed to get in touch with four wireless operators of an East Prussian unit, where his activities caused a great deal of trouble. After two years he was dismissed by the Poles as being of no further use to them and emigrated to America. Twelve years later he returned to Germany, where he was recognized by a police officer, arrested and sentenced to fifteen years' penal servitude. He died in prison of tuberculosis.

Throughout this period, the Intelligence Service suffered from a lack of funds. Up to 1933 the authorized annual expenditure stood at about a million marks, in other words about five thousand pounds sterling a month—far too small a sum for the maintenance of the Central Office and its seven subsidiaries. Quality rather than quantity was therefore the rule; the Abwehr worked with a few, but good, men. Care, however, had to be taken not to over-pay even these good men, for any agent who becomes conspicuous through lavish expenditure is very swiftly rendered innocuous. In spite of this, two good agents were lost for this very reason. They were both men in comparatively subordinate positions who, thanks to the lax manner in which the Poles safeguarded their files, had access to papers dealing with the naval stations of Hela and Oxthoeft. The money they earned was promptly transformed into schnapps, and that was the end of them. In the course of three years of service one of them had been paid no less than one hundred and sixty thousand sloty for himself and his sources, and every sloty of it was money well spent.

When the Polish campaign began, the picture of the Polish Army and the Polish mobilization scheme was complete, and there was nothing more for Abwehr Sub-Section East to do.

Thanks to the rapidity of the German advance, the 'spiderweb' which had been organized beforehand was not called upon to function, and not one of the wireless stations set up in Poland itself was able to contribute anything of importance for the further information of the invading armies. The task of the Abwehr had been fulfilled completely.

The period of crisis which immediately preceded the outbreak of war was utilized by the Intelligence Service to secure bases in the Scandinavian area, from which to ensure as complete an observation of shipping movements in the North Sea as possible. In the principal western ports of Bergen, Stavenger, Christiansand, Oslo, Gotenburg and Skagen experienced observers were installed, who were in daily touch with their command post in Germany, and this system was expanded during the winter of 1939/40 to a degree which ensured an almost complete coverage of all shipping movements. Of vital importance to the German Supreme Command were reports regarding the composition and dates of sailing of convoys bound for Britain. These reports gradually became so precise, accurate and speedily transmitted, that the Commander of Air Corps X in Hamburg was able, weather permitting, to launch his attacks with the utmost precision and with great success. During that winter more than 150,000 tons were sunk as the direct result of these reports.

The sailing time of these convoys was usually fixed only a few hours before the convoy departed, and precise reports on sailing times could only be sent by German agents during the night before sailing hour. At this time the number of seagoing submarines was too small to permit of the necessary continuous watch on the relevant ports, and action by other units of the Navy was precluded by the time and distance factors involved. The task of attacking the convoys was therefore assigned exclusively to the Air Arm.

As early as November 1939 Admiral Raeder proposed to Hitler that an expedition be sent against Norway; nothing, however, was done about it from the Intelligence point of view, nor was any reconnaissance ordered. Suddenly, in the latter half of January 1940, a report was received by the Hamburg Abwehr station that the Chasseurs Alpins were being withdrawn from the Metz sector of the French front for transportation to Britain and subsequent action in North Europe. The importance of the report was enhanced by the fact that it came from an agent of proved reliability; and in spite of the closing of the Franco-German frontier and the agent's lack of any form of wireless communication, it had reached Hamburg within four days of dispatch—a proof of the efficiency of the lines of communication which had been previously prepared before the war.

The Intelligence Officer of the Hamburg station responsible has given the following account:

'At the end of February 1940 I was suddenly ordered to proceed to Berlin, where I was to report to Commando zbV 31, a newly-raised organization of which I had never heard; its offices were on the top floor of the buildings occupied by Supreme Headquarters, Armed Forces, on the corner of the Tirpitzufer and Bendlerstrasse and were the object of special and very strict security measures.

'By the General Staff Officer in charge I was told that I was to submit within four weeks a precise military reconnaissance report on Denmark. I might mention that hitherto no military reconnaissance of Denmark had ever been made. Under special oath of secrecy I was then informed of the intentions of the Supreme Command, which were to culminate in April in the occupation of Denmark and Norway. Although I could not confirm it, I had the impression that our reports on the transfer of the Chasseurs Alpins to Britain had something to do with these activities.

'I returned to Hamburg and forthwith set about preparations for the accomplishment of the task allotted me. The first thing to be done was to find out the exact Order of Battle of the Danish Army. To complete my task within so short a period

I had to call into activity certain dormant liaison agents in Denmark. These agents had originally been designed to act as links, in neutral Danish territory, in our lines of communication with other neutral and potential enemy countries against the outbreak of a war and the closing of the frontiers. Next, I sent agents to various districts with orders to ascertain and record, according to the formation and the branch of the Service to which they belonged, the units of the Danish Army stationed in the districts allotted to them. A further important point which had to be settled was whether the Danish Armed Forces had mined the principal roads of entry at the frontier or taken any other special security measures against a possible invasion. Up to the very moment of invasion the Danish Intelligence Service remained in complete ignorance of these reconnaissance activities, and all my agents returned safely to Germany.

'Eventually and after four weeks of incessant work, night and day, I was able to submit to Supreme Headquarters a complete picture of the distribution of the Danish land forces.

'In order to ensure both that the results of this reconnaissance were fully available to the troops taking part in the enterprise on April 9th, 1940 and that the vanguards of the invading columns were in possession of precise information regarding the distribution of the Danish forces, I decided, without any particular order from Berlin, to place intelligence officers of the Danish Section of the Hamburg Abwehr station at the dispoals of the invading columns. The officer in charge of Sub-Section, Army Reconnaissance was attached to the I.C. A/O. of the Special Duty Commando, and an officer with a Commando escort was attached to each of the two invading columns—that in the west, which was to enter Denmark via Tondern, and that in the east which was to go in via Flensburg. This was the first occasion on which a service of this nature was rendered by the Intelligence Service to the fighting forces. The formation, a little later, of front line Intelligence Commandos in all army groups is the best proof of the importance of the services rendered.

'While the reconnaissance of Denmark was entrusted to home intelligence stations, as described above, the reconnaissance of Norway had to be left for the most part to the KOs. (War Organizations) in that country. It was, however, considered desirable to organize other possible sources of information to supplement the efforts of the War Organizations, and in this respect the services of the German mercantile navy could be of great value. As I already knew the date of X-Day, for the invasion, my first preoccupation was to find out which merchant ships would probably be arriving in south Norwegian ports—the focal point of the invasion—during the second week in April, and to arrange with them for the collection and onward transmission of reports. As it had to be assumed that in the event of war the normal wireless installation of German ships in Norwegian harbours would be forthwith sealed by the port authorities and kept under surveillance, it was necessary to provide these ships with a special, secret transmitter, and for this purpose I decided to use the A.F.U. transmitter, an apparatus issued to agents and built into a small suitcase which could be used independently of the ship's installation.

'By a most happy chance, the steamship *Vidar* was in Oslo harbour on the day of the invasion. As the first of the Luftwaffe squadrons landed at Hornebu, the Oslo airport, early in the morning, a man suddenly appeared on board the *Vidar* and identified himself as a member of the Abwehr from Berlin. His first question was: "Have you people got an A.F.U. set aboard?" When the wireless operator who had been lent to the ship by the Hamburg Intelligence station said that he had, the man immediately assumed control, and in a few minutes contact was established with the Hamburg wireless station. In the hours that followed the Abwehr man sent off message after message, at intervals of minutes, at first in cipher and later *en clair*, giving what was almost a running commentary on the landing of German aircraft and the counter-measures being taken by the Norwegians. Between the landing of the first

85

planes and the late afternoon some 250 reports were received in Hamburg, and were sent on from there at once to Abwehr Headquarters and thence direct to Supreme Headquarters.

'About an hour after the receipt of the first message a direct telephone call came through to Hamburg from Supreme Head-quarters, asking whence these reports were originating. I very soon found out that these were the first reports received at Headquarters on the situation in Norway and that throughout that first momentous day our reports were far more accurate and precise than any sent by the Military Headquarters com-manding the operations; indeed, in the course of the morning, the time taken for a message from the *Vidar* to reach Supreme Headquarters was reduced to as little as seven minutes!'

The occupation of Copenhagen was carried out by German troops landing at dawn from a German merchant ship lying in the harbour. Their first action was to seize the only two approaches to a fortress outside the town in which the whole communication system of the Danish Armed Forces was con-centrated. This was swiftly accomplished, and with the fort entirely cut off, the channel for the passing of orders to the Danish Army was at once paralysed; news of the German invasion could not be sent out, nor could any orders be given for the organization of resistance. As a result, the occupation of Denmark was completed without bloodshed.

The officer responsible for the preliminary reconnaissance of Copenhagen and for suggesting this plan of operation had made a particular point of carrying out a thorough reconnaissance of this communication centre. He had been inspired to do so by the reading of a book on the technique of *coups d'état* by the Italian writer, Malaparte. This work was on the proscribed list in Germany, but the officer in question had managed to get hold of a copy. One chapter described the seizure of St. Petersburg by the Bolsheviks under Lenin and Trotsky. Lenin had insisted that the masses should demonstrate and seize the important points in the city. To Trotsky this appeared to be of minor importance; nevertheless he agreed, but only after he had assured himself that he would be able beforehand to ensure a total and timely severance of all communication between the city itself and the neighbouring barracks.

In general it seems to me that the activities of the Abwehr in preparing for the Danish and Norwegian operations were among the most successful that were carried out. Time was short, the situation was complicated, and in the case of Norway, distances were considerable, yet all went without a hitch. Thus by the spring of 1940 the Abwehr had won its spurs in two campaigns of very different natures. It was functioning smoothly and efficiently and was ready for its biggest task so far, the Campaign in the West.

THE rapid and thorough jobs done by the Abwehr in the weeks immediately preceding the occupation of Denmark and Norway were, in many ways, models of improvisation and of initiative. They were also highly effective. But they were comparatively small in scope and brief in time. As an example of a long-range and large-scale operation by the German Intelligence the preparations against France in particular and the Western powers in general are of far greater significance. And though in some ways comparable with the Abwehr activities in Poland, they were far larger and far more complicated, eventually involving as they did every branch of the Abwehr. There was, in particular, one vital element here present which was absent from the Polish operation.

Intelligence activity as regards Poland was a typical example of an intelligence service working against a country which was of military importance, but which was devoid of any practical naval significance. In addition, it was also activity against a country which was joined to Germany by a long land frontier. It is true that in the West France and Germany have a very extensive common land frontier, but the remaining countries were not directly accessible, with the exception of Holland and Belgium, and against these latter two no organized intelligence service was set up. They were to be used more or less as 'host-countries'—as bases, that is, for activity against others—but not of themselves to be regarded as fields for reconnaissance, nor, indeed, was it thought that they should ever be taken into consideration as potential enemies. All the other countries in the West were of both military and naval interest, and how the Intelligence activities against them were organized is described by an officer who for many years was engaged in Naval Intelligence in this theatre.

'In January 1934 I was posted to the Abwehr station of Naval North Sea Command in Wilhelmshaven. The station, for all practical purposes, had neither agents nor any channels of communication. It had a subsidiary branch in Hamburg in which one further representative was engaged in intelligence work. Originally the Wilhelmshaven station's sole task was the organization in Holland and Belgium of a network of informers able to bring information in the event of any crisis or mobilization in any other country, and particularly in France and Great Britain. Spade-work of this kind is hardly ever a satisfying sort of employment; the potential informers enlisted in case of need remain devoid of any sort of training, and when a crisis actually occurs, they usually fail to accomplish the task allotted to them.

'One lucky coincidence brought a little animation into this otherwise somewhat forlorn picture. One day two merchant seamen came to the Abwehr station and presented us with the blueprints of an instrument destined for the American Air Force which they had picked up somewhere or other in the United States. They had no idea either of the purpose or the significance of the instrument, but the blueprint certainly appeared to be genuine. The American Army and Navy, as such, were at the time of no particular interest to the German Intelligence Service; but information regarding technical advances, which were then occurring at frequent and short intervals in foreign armed forces and which might well be of use to the German forces, were, of course, of the greatest possible interest. In Germany itself naval construction was severely restricted by the terms of the Versailles Treaty, while aircraft construction was completely forbidden. On the other hand security and the safeguarding of secrets in the United States were extremely lax, and skilful agents had little difficulty in penetrating important construction and industrial centres and in finding out a good deal more about methods of production than was ever made public; and although a study of American publications normally gave a very good insight into the trend of technical progress, it failed to give the ultimate, precise information which can only be obtained through trial and error. In the course of time, however, we were able in this way to obtain designs of new aircraft, bombing apparatus and instruments of a similar nature, and finally to get hold of a whole series of blueprints and drawings of various new types of destroyers and battleships and even the secret instructions governing their construction.

'When Admiral Canaris took over command of the Intelligence Service in 1935 he directed that the station be transferred from Wilhelmshaven, which he regarded as "simply an armed forces' canteen" and quite unsuitable as a base for the conduct of Intelligence activities, to another big town nearby. Under the new and more favourable conditions which then came into being it was possible to initiate via Holland and Belgium (the so-called Northern France route) a systematic Intelligence survey of the French Navy, as far at least as the Channel and the Atlantic seaboard were concerned. This included reconnaissance of coastal defences, naval dockyards and commercial ports and their respective capacities, as well as types and methods of construction of warships, with details of their construction, armour and armaments, torpedo tubes, mine-laying apparatus, anti-submarine devices, anti-aircraft weapons and so on. Finally, information was sought as to the precise whereabouts both of naval aircraft stations and of aerodromes in the immediate coastal districts, as well as details of supplies of fue oil for the French Navy and Army, and the whereabouts and capacities of oil refineries and their importance, not only as sources of supply for the French armed forces, but also as targets, should the necessity arise, for our own Air Force.

'To fulfil these tasks we had slowly and laboriously to enlist and build up a network of agents, most of whom, however, were not Frenchmen, but men of various other nationalities. These were then put through a rigorous course of training at the Intelligence Centre, in which the importance of the particular district in which each man was to work was pointed out and the general principles of reconnaissance methods to be followed as regards the layout of fortifications, the methods of ship construction, economic questions such as the supply and demand for oil and so on were fully and carefully explained. As a general rule, it is men imbued with a love of adventure who allow themselves to be enlisted for work of this kind; indeed, many such need no persuasion, but voluntarily offer their services, and it is essential that the officer in charge of them and of their instruction should succeed in establishing an atmosphere of mutual confidence; on his side, the officer must be convinced that he can trust his agents, and they on the other hand must be equally sure that they can rely absolutely on their officer's assistance, should they ever find themselves in difficulties. This atmosphere of mutual trust cannot be achieved by money alone. Admiral Canaris himself attached great importance to avoiding methods which might lead to pressure or blackmail being brought to bear on agents. He also forbade the use of so-called *agents provocateurs*, and in these matters he was inexorable and reacted with the utmost severity against any disobedience of his instructions. It was, indeed, his wish to see the Intelligence Service run in an honourable and decent fashion.

'This reconnaissance of the French coastal areas was gradually extended with success to include also the southern coast of France.

'Apart from the long-range work outlined above, reconnaissance was also carried out from the West of Germany and from the South via Spain. The Maginot Line, as a defensive system of primary importance, was, of course, the principal object of our endeavours. The defection of Frogé of the French Commissariat Department led to a court case which aroused great interest for a long while in both the French and the foreign press. He was responsible for supplying rations to the troops in the Maginot Line and had placed his extensive knowledge at the disposal of the German authorities. Apart from this, much valuable material was found when Prague was occupied in 1938. The Czech defensive system against Germany had been constructed with French assistance on the model of the Maginot Line, and in this connection a Czech technical commission had visited the French defences and returned with many detailed drawings and specifications. The military co-operation between Czechoslovakia, a member of the Little Entente, and France was, in the nature of things, very close, and the fruits thereof—to the great advantage of the German Intelligence Service—were found in the safes of Section II of the Czechoslovakian General Staff.

'Initially all Intelligence work against Great Britain was forbidden, and it was only in 1936 that this ruling was somewhat relaxed and a certain measure of observation activity was permitted; even then, however, the employment of regular agents was denied to us. But in the autumn of 1937 these restrictions were removed, and we were given full liberty of action, not only in the United Kingdom itself, but also for the collation of reports on naval stations and bases overseas. The enlistment of agents capable of covering so vast an area offered enormous difficulties; but by the time war was declared, we had succeeded in obtaining most of the really important information concerning the Royal Navy which we required, though our dossier was not nearly as complete as that dealing with the French Navy and its various naval stations.

'The placing of agents in Britain itself was extremely difficult. The British were in a position to exercise a far more efficient system of supervision over all foreigners entering their island than is possible in the case of a country with a land frontier. Apart from this, a passionate desire to play the amateur detective is a characteristic common to all classes of Britons, and it is not merely coincidence that Conan Doyle, the father of modern detective stories, and Edgar Wallace are both Britons and vastly superior to the authors of detective fiction in other lands. The average Briton, too, views all foreigners with a measure of distrust, however polite he may be to them in his normal daily intercourse.

'A problem to which Canaris himself—and consequently the

whole of the Intelligence Service—gave particular study was the devising of means to ensure that the transmission of reports should not be interrupted in times of tension and mobilization, and above all that agents employed upon other tasks should be meticulously trained and told exactly what they had to do, when any crisis arose. Every agent, whose employment in a period of crisis was envisaged, was furnished with a personal code-word, on receipt of which he would be required forthwith to abandon any activity on which he was engaged and go at once to a specified district, in which he was to visit a previously arranged series of places whence, via lines of communication also previously arranged and in camouflaged phraseology, he would send in his reports on preparations for war.

'This system came into action for the first time in 1936, when the Rhineland was reoccupied. Although the period of preparation at its disposal before it was called upon to operate had been very short, the network functioned excellently, and the military High Command was given a timely and trustworthy picture of the measures being taken by neighbouring armies and navies as a result of the reoccupation.

'The same procedure was used on two subsequent occasions —the occupation of Austria and the Sudeten crisis. The march into Austria was planned to occur on a Saturday. On the previous Thursday, the chiefs of all intelligence stations were suddenly ordered to report immediately to Canaris, who told them that Hitler had decided to march into Austria and to settle the Austrian problem, if necessary by force. Both the gravity of the occasion and the extreme anxiety of the Admiral were apparent to all present. The intelligence stations worked day and night, all the necessary instructions were issued, and the Service sat back to await reports; and reports they certainly got, reports which were almost unanimous in stating that reactions and counter-measures of any importance were negligible in all neighbouring States. The Service had functioned admirably, and the Intelligence network set up for periods of crisis and mobilization had given a true and accurate picture of the situation. By the time the Sudeten crisis arose, the system had been considerably improved and it worked at least as well as on the previous occasion, if not better.

'In the year 1938 we achieved some outstanding successes, but also suffered some resounding setbacks. Of the latter, one occurred in the United States and was due in no small measure to the fact that in the meanwhile the Secret State Police—the Gestapo—which in reality was a purely internal organization, had thrust its way into Intelligence activities abroad—a state of affairs that was in direct contravention of the agreement reached between Canaris and Heydrich, the Gestapo Chief. Further, at about this time a remarkable psychosis developed in the Third Reich, whose nationals became obsessed with the belief that by pouring in reports from abroad of any and every description which seemed to them to be of importance, they would be serving the interests of their fatherland. Nor did it stop at that; a whole host of individuals suddenly discovered that they possessed exceptional talents for Intelligence work and felt impelled to dedicate themselves to Intelligence activities. Amateurs of this kind invariably become immediately conspicuous, because they always have so fatally exaggerated an opinion of their own importance as the guardians of weighty secrets and the servants of a great mission. Their whole demeanour immediately betrays them, and, as often as not, they succeed in drawing attention to themselves long before they manage even to approach a goal which is of the slightest importance from the Intelligence point of view.

'The United States of America was the happy hunting ground *in excelsis* of these enthusiastic cranks, and from there they poured in their reports—to the Overseas Branch of the National Socialist Party, to the *Arbeitsfront* (the Labour Organization), to the German Ministry of Aviation, and even sometimes to the German State Railways, all of which organizations had their own representatives in the United States.

'As early as 1936 or 1937 an agent of Section I (Air) of the Abwehr had been unmasked as a spy by the Americans and only with the greatest difficulty and the help of friends had he escaped by car to Canada and thence to Germany. As a result of this case the F.B.I. (Federal Bureau of Investigation) increased its vigilance very considerably, and its interest was focused primarily on the "Bund der Freunde des neuen Deutschlands" (The Association of Friends of New Germany). My office and its employees had been warned again and again against this organization and against making any contact with any of its leaders. In view of the great distances involved and the limitations inherent in the courier system of communication in force, anything approaching effective control was to all practical purposes impossible. Most unfortunately at about this time one of our couriers, a man whose four years of trustworthy service had inspired justifiable confidence, came under the influence of a certain Rumrich, a Sudeten German living in the United States.

'This Rumrich produced the most fantastic plans, and he succeeded in persuading the hitherto reliable agent to collaborate, on his own responsibility, in an undertaking in the United States of which we in Germany knew nothing. He had conceived the idea of enticing a senior officer of the American Army—the Commandant, say, of some fortress or other—to meet him in some bar and of there persuading him to hand over the mobilization scheme of the fortress and units under his command. He procured some official note-paper and envelopes from the War Department and wrote to the officer of his choice, directing him to meet a representative of that Department in a certain public house and to hand over to him the schemes and plans enumerated in the letter. He himself proposed to play the part of the War Department representative. The selected officer duly appeared at the time and place appointed—and with him were officials of the F.B.I., who promptly arrested Rumrich. In the subsequent interrogation Rumrich immediately gave away a whole list of names, and it became apparent that he had indeed succeeded in organizing a complete "grape-vine". As it happened, the confidential courier of the Abwehr was at that moment on leave outside the United States. Without the knowledge of his superior officer, he had enlisted as locum tenens a woman hairdresser of the liner *Europa*, to whom he had given full instructions, and had then proceeded on leave. Faced with a *fait accompli*, his superior officer had no alternative, if the courier service was to remain in uninterrupted action, but to employ the woman and make the best of it. This acting courier was, of course, known to Rumrich, and hers was one of the first names he betrayed. When the *Europa* next berthed in New York, the hairdresser Johanna Hoffmann was arrested as she stepped ashore, and all the mail which she was carrying was seized. She, too, immediately told all she knew; despite the assurance of the real courier to the contrary, she was aware not only of this particular channel of communication but of several others too, and so the result was a whole crop of further arrests.

'Among those arrested were a well-known New York doctor and his mistress. The lady in question was swiftly released, and the doctor, too, was given a warning and restored to a freedom of which he at once took advantage to flee to Germany as a stowaway on a German ship. The American authorities tried to hold up the vessel when it was clear of the three-mile limit, but the Captain refused to stop and the doctor reached Germany in safety. A further number of people implicated in the affair also succeeded in fleeing to Germany; they had, however, nothing to do with the German Military Intelligence Service, but had become involved either as mutual acquaintances in the grape-vine mentioned above or with the other various organizations which had thrust a meddlesome finger in the Intelligence pie. Even so, for weeks afterwards the headlines of the American Press read: "NAZI SPIES IN AMERICA" . . . "THE NAZI SPY HUNT IS ON!" The whole episode assumed enormous proportions, and eighteen people, among them the German officers Colonel Busch, Lieut.-Commander Menzel, Captain von Bonin and Captain Pheiffer, were charged. The case has been described in a book written by an F.B.I. official, Leon G. Turrou, which admittedly makes exciting reading, but which shows that the F.B.I. had failed to grasp the confused situation, and did not realize that only a small proportion of the persons accused were in fact working for German military intelligence.

'The inevitable result of this case, which dragged on from March until the summer of 1938, was that in our activities against the United States we had to be extremely circumspect and mark time. Later, with increased security measures, work was resumed; a whole team of agents worked consistently according to the orders of the officer in charge of them, regarding themselves as individual workers and not as members of some such grape-vine as has been described above, and this continued to give satisfactory results right up to the outbreak of war.'

But far more important in the days before the war were the preparations against France. And it was in France and the Low Countries, in the summer of 1940, that the Abwehr which Canaris had built up and trained was truly put to the test. It was here that Abwehr II first really went into action in support of a major military operation.

In the planning for the surprise invasion of Holland, Belgium and Luxembourg, a major preoccupation was whether it would be possible to seize the bridges over the Maas and the Albert Canal intact. Only if that could be done would the army be able swiftly to reach the Peel position in Holland and thereafter quickly relieve the paratroops dropped in the vicinity of Rotterdam.

In November 1939 a conference on the subject was held in the Reich Chancellery with Hitler presiding. As a result the Abwehr was ordered to prepare a plan for the seizure, by means of a *ruse de guerre*—by troops, that is, dressed in Dutch and Belgian uniforms—of the most important bridges over the Maas, the two road and one railway bridge at Maastricht and the one road and one railway bridge at Gennep.

Early in the preparations a most annoying setback was experienced. The agent who had been detailed to procure pattern uniforms was captured by the Belgians with the uniforms in his possession. In connection with this mysterious theft of uniforms a Flemish newspaper published a caricature of Goering, wearing the uniform of a Brussels tram conductor and admiring himself in a mirror, with the caption: 'This does suit me well!'

It is quite astonishing that this episode aroused no suspicions either in Holland or Belgium, and that no additional precautionary instructions were as a result issued to the frontier guards. Had the Dutch realized, for instance, what the significance of this abuse of their uniforms was to have been, they would have been spared the surprise overthrow they suffered at Gennep and might have caused a delay in the German advance, which, while it would probably not have affected the fate of the western campaign, might well have led to the cutting off of the air-borne troops landed behind the Dutch lines.

The operations against the Maastricht bridges were not carried out by the Brandenburg Regiment, but by a volunteer unit of Sub-station Breslau (Special Duty Battalion 100). An advance guard, dressed in uniforms surrendered by Dutchmen, drove in the early hours of May 10th, 1940 via Raedern and Sittart to Maastricht. What happened next is not generally known. The only certainty appears to be that one of the road bridges leading to Maastricht was seized, but the detonating charge could not be removed. After a wild shooting affray, in which the Commander of the bogus Dutchmen, Lieutenant Hocke, lost his life, all three bridges blew up. The Maastricht enterprise had ended in complete failure, and it was a depressing sight for the Abwehr chief when on his arrival a few hours later he found whole columns of tanks and lorries jammed on the roads leading to Maastricht and waiting impatiently until the Engineer Corps had thrown a field-service bridge across the river. For it was precisely to avoid this loss of time in the blitz attack that the Maastricht operation had been devised.

The success of the operation at Gennep, carried out by a unit of the Brandenburg Special Duty Battalion 800 under the command of Lieutenant Walther, however, more or less counter-balanced the failure at Maastricht; and as soon as he heard that the Gennep bridges had been secured intact, General von Reichenau, the Commander-in-Chief of the Sixth Army forcing its way through the narrow gap between Roermond and Liége, was able immediately to divert some of the units stuck fast at Maastricht to the Gennep route.

This Gennep enterprise was most carefully planned and was executed in partial camouflage. A reconnaissance platoon, disguised as German prisoners under Dutch escort, seized the bridge well before zero hour, and, before the Dutch could recover from their surprise, a column of German tanks was rolling across this important Meuse crossing. The 'prisoners' were men of the Brandenburg Regiment, with hand-grenades and automatic pistols concealed under their greatcoats. And the 'escort' were agents from the Flemish nationalist, Mussert movement, disguised as men of the Dutch Frontier Guards. The gaining of a purely military objective by Secret Service methods—in other words, the tactical co-ordination of the action of regular troops and agents—was successfully employed for the first time in this Gennep affair.

While Abwehr Section II helped to open the gateway into enemy territory for the invading armies, Section I assumed responsibility for field reconnaissance and accompanied the van of the advance. The following account has been given of its activities:

'On May 10th, zero day for the Western campaign, Lieut.-Commander Kilwen was ordered to organize a naval Abwehr Commando in Cologne, and take it to join the forces invading Holland. With the exception of the activities of Abwehr III's Commandos, which had taken part in the Polish campaign and were now accompanying the troops in Holland, there was nothing to guide Commander Kilwen as to the composition and armament of the unit he was to raise. Its orders were to press on with those units of the invading forces which had been detailed for the capture of ports and coastal towns, and there to seize all material of an Intelligence character, examine it and sort it as quickly as possible and forward at once anything of immediate tactical value to the military headquarters directing operations. The rest of the material was then to be taken to the nearest landing-ground and flown to Abwehr Headquarters in Berlin.

'From this it was obvious that the provision of a very adequate number of motor-cars was the first essential. The Commando was also reinforced by a motorized platoon of the Secret Field Police and a wireless operator equipped with an A.F.U. agent's wireless set. During its advance, the Commando's task was further enlarged by an order to set up at once in each important port a small detachment to act as a Secret Intelligence report group. Within three days, on May 13th, the Commando began its advance and it went into action for the first time in the Rotterdam area, reaching the town itself at the same time as the advancing regular troops. Particular importance was attached to the seizure of examples of the degaussing apparatus, an invention which was said to neutralize the action of the German magnetic mine. A number of these contrivances were found on various ships, dismantled and sent back; and at one wharf the plan for the construction of the whole apparatus was found.

'Making Rotterdam its headquarters for the time being, the Commando sent one platoon to be present at the capture of Den Helder and another with the troops advancing on Antwerp. In both these places secret intelligence report groups were set up, as ordered. The Commando was then attached to the Fourth Army, to the headquarters of which it proceeded via Brussels and Maubeuge, whence it accompanied von Kleist's army in its advance on the Channel ports.

'For some astonishing reason the French defenders destroyed neither their archives nor even the various papers in the military vehicles stranded in the shallow water near the beaches, and in Boulogne and other ports a mass of most valuable material was captured. In a British R.A.F. station the cipher in use between the British and French armies, complete with the key for May and June 1940, fell into German hands.

'The further advance led first to Calais and Dunkirk, then south-westwards to Le Tréport, Dieppe, St. Valéry, Le Havre and Rouen, and finally to Brest and as far south as Rochefort. In the meanwhile the archives of the French Ministry of Marine in Paris had fallen into German hands.

'When the armistice with France was concluded, Brest became the principal intelligence station, the tentacles of which stretched into unoccupied France, North Africa, the Iberian peninsula and Britain itself. An Abwehr Section II group was ordered to try to penetrate into England and plant saboteurs there. The great hopes which were centred on the Brest station were not, however, realized. What Canaris had once most aptly said about Wilhelmshaven applied with equal force to Brest—"You can't run a secret intelligence service from an Armed Forces Canteen." '

Much has been said about the activities of the Abwehr in Ireland, most of which is grossly exaggerated or simply untrue. Until shortly before the outbreak of war German policy envisaged friendly relations with the British Empire. With this end in view, Abwehr II was categorically forbidden to have any dealings with the Irish Republican Army either in Eire, Ulster, Great Britain or the U.S.A. Although the Abwehr had collected a certain amount of information about Ireland from agents visiting that country, it was militarily of no value.

In the months immediately preceding the war, however, contact was established with a leading personality in the Irish economy, a man who though not publicly connected with the Irish Republican movement was believed to have access to its leaders. At the outbreak of war this contact was still too loose for the personage in question to be used as a means for the mutual exchange of information. The Abwehr therefore sent an agent, via a neutral country, to London. This man was to pass

102

the necessary codes and so on to the Irishman, for it was hoped that eventually a wireless link could be established between Ireland and Germany. In fact it is quite impractical to attempt to set up a wireless link in this fashion, and the Abwehr had to rely on verbal and written reports passed through its own agents visiting Ireland via neutral countries. Throughout the course of the war only a single Irish courier ever reached Germany.

In general it may be said that though the leaders of the Irish Republican movement were prepared, throughout the war, to collaborate with the Germans, they were not prepared to take orders from Germany. At this time the I.R.A. had been weakened by the wave of sabotage and propaganda activities in which it had indulged in 1938, principally in Liverpool and London, since a high proportion of its most active and capable members had been arrested and were now in prison. The Germans were therefore anxious that what strength it possessed should be devoted to military, rather than politico-propaganda activities.

With this aim in mind it was decided to send Captain Dr. Goertz, an officer of Abwehr II, to Ireland. He was to be liaison officer between Abwehr II and the command staff of the I.R.A. in Southern Ireland. He was given wide discretionary powers and within the aims outlined above was free to act as he saw fit. One of his tasks, however, was to establish if he could a wireless link with Berlin.

His mission was an almost total failure. He landed by parachute, but by mistake in Northern, not Southern, Ireland. He lost his radio equipment, which was on another parachute. He was within an ace of being captured by the Royal Ulster Constabulary. When, after a perilous journey, he at last established contact with the I.R.A. in Eire, it was only to discover that that organization was riven with enmity. Indeed his time was so fully taken up in ensuring that the opposition group within the I.R.A. did not betray him to the Free State authorities, that he could not begin to carry out his military tasks.

The whole business reduced Dr. Goertz to a state of nervous prostration and he set about attempting to secure a passage back to Germany. He failed, was in due course arrested by the police and interned. It says a great deal for the seriousness with which he regarded his mission and for his loyalty to his true colleagues within the I.R.A. that he committed suicide when at last the Irish Government, surrendering to heavy diplomatic pressure, agreed to hand him over to the Anglo-Americans.

The Abwehr was slightly, though not much, more successful with the Irish in America. The I.R.A. had a tight and efficient organization on the Eastern seaboard, its members were well trained—particularly in sabotage—and were commanded by a former chief of staff of the whole I.R.A., Sean Russell. He came to Germany, via Genoa, in April 1940 as a stowaway on board the American liner *George Washington*. The United States were getting too hot for him, and also he wished to organize collaboration with the Germans. The Abwehr established contact with his people in America via the Abwehr unit in Mexico, which was in the competent hands of a German businessman. But it soon transpired that the American I.R.A. was not only anti-British but also strongly anti-capitalist. Like their colleagues in Ireland, they quite refused to accept instructions from Germany. Indeed they deliberately acted contrary to German wishes, which at that time were to avoid an entanglement with the United States. The German Foreign Office absolutely forbade any sabotage in the United States, but the I.R.A. ignored this and did their best to blow up British ships and to damage factories working for the British. Later the Abwehr unit in Mexico had to be closed down for security reasons. With the outbreak of hostilities between Germany and the U.S.S.R. the anti-capitalist bias within the American I.R.A. made all prospects of collaboration between that organization and Germany fruitless.

The former chief of staff of the I.R.A. remained in Berlin, as a protégé of the Foreign Office. The German plans for the invasion of England did not, as is known, involve a simultaneous descent upon Ireland. But it was believed that as the battle in Great Britain developed, the British would probably occupy the Free State. The presence of the former I.R.A. chief of staff therefore assumed some importance at this time; indeed it was his high-water mark. In the event of a British invasion of Eire, it was the intention of the Germans to support an expected Irish resistance movement with all the means available short of the actual dispatch of troops. This, it was believed, would produce the maximum benefit to the German cause. The ex-chief of staff was therefore sent to Ireland, by U-boat, to make the necessary preparations. However, even this came to nothing, since the man died of a burst stomach ulcer on board ship and was buried at sea; the U-boat returned to Lorient.

After the abandonment of Operation Sea-Lion Germany's chief interest in Ireland was that that country should remain neutral. With this end in view all Abwehr activities were strictly curtailed and at one time forbidden. However, when the Battle of the Atlantic reached its crisis in 1942, and the value of the Irish ports was being strongly felt in England, there seemed once again to be a risk of a British invasion. The Germans now had as their adviser on Eirean affairs a well-known Irish politician who had had a spectacular career, having been at one time a senior officer in the Spanish Republican International Brigade; captured and condemned to death by Franco, which sentence was later commuted to thirty years' imprisonment, he had been released owing to the intervention of Admiral Canaris in 1940 and brought to Germany. He was a tragically impractical man and before the end of the war he, too, was dead; his health had been broken by his sufferings in the Spanish war and in the Spanish prisons.

The activities of Abwehr II in Ireland during the second world war were thus, as will have been seen, quite insignificant and without any military effect on the course of the war. The reason is not far to seek, quite apart from repeated bad luck

105

as exemplified in Dr. Goertz's being dropped in the wrong place, the death of the ex-I.R.A. chief of staff and so on. Abwehr II, with its strictly military mission, found itself continually at loggerheads with the Foreign Office, which of course acted from political motives. The Foreign Office effectively stymied all the plans of Abwehr II. However, this is no criticism of the Foreign Office: the whole course of the second world war shows how essential it is that military plans should play second fiddle to political decisions.

So much for the role of Abwehr II in the West. After the fall of France, and during the preparations for Operation Sea-Lion Abwehr Section III also found itself for the time being with very little that was of real importance to do, for at first there was no sign of any attempt at spying or sabotage by the opponents. The French population seemed dazed by the shock of events. But the 'I spy a spy' complex of the troops themselves gave a tremendous amount of work; acts of sabotage were seen in every conceivable type of everyday occurrence and the Abwehr officers were for ever on the run, confirming, investigating and holding urgent conferences with the different commanders and their staffs. Particularly numerous were reports of sabotage against telegraph lines and of mysterious lights and signals; but nearly all of them proved to have a perfectly innocent explanation.

Fresh tasks arose in the late summer of 1940, when that part of the old Commando which was still mobile moved to Paris and was attached to Army Group A at St. Germain, where it was directed to proceed with the organization of the Abwehr Commando for Operation Sea-Lion, the invasion of Britain. For this operation Supreme Headquarters proposed to use two assault armies, the Eighteenth Army and the Ninth Army, with the Sixth Army as a follow-up. Each army was to be supplied with an Abwehr Commando for active reconnaissance and an Abwehr Section III Commando to combat the activities of the enemy Intelligence Service. Particular attention was paid to wireless communications and to maps, town plans, plans of wharves and other similar installations, which had been collected well in advance and which would now be of great importance to the armies in their advance.

When Operation Sea-Lion was finally abandoned in the late autumn of 1940, the Brest station resumed its former activities. In the meanwhile the effects of the initial shock which had so dazed the French had been dissipated; demobilized French soldiers had returned to their homes, and the more spirited and enterprising among them began to strive to join the Free French forces under de Gaulle. Large numbers tried to reach England from the small Breton harbours in fishing boats, and not a few of them felt that it was their duty to arrive, not empty-handed, but with such information about the German occupation forces, their distribution and armament, as they could collect. In the opposite direction the de Gaullist Intelligence Service strove also to penetrate into France through these French ports. The control of the innumerable little hamlets dotted along the far-flung, rocky and broken coast of Brittany became a problem of primary importance; a dense network of coast and harbour guards and patrols had to be organized, and this was supplemented by the formation of the 'Augmented Coastal Frontier Supervision Force', a species of militarized Customs Department, with its headquarters in Paris, officered entirely by reserve officers of the old and new Wehrmacht and manned exclusively by ex-soldiers. This organization co-operated in the most loyal manner with the Abwehr.

It was towards the turn of the year 1940/41 that these new measures scored their first success, when a group was captured trying to reach England with very comprehensive reports on the German occupation forces and the Channel fortifications; shortly afterwards a trawler fell into German hands near Brest, aboard which were two British agents, equipped with wireless. They had been picked up at sea at one of the rendezvous points, at which the Breton fishermen used to meet their fellows who had succeeded in escaping to England and to pass

107

across reports and agents. The sardine and tunny-fish trawlers had a radius of action of a hundred sea miles and could remain at sea for days on end. The simplest solution, of course, would have been to forbid all fishing or to restrict it to the immediate and visible vicinity of the coast; but such drastic action would have resulted in severe losses of valuable food.

German officers stationed in occupied France are agreed that the activities of the de Gaullist Intelligence Service were conducted in a decent and gentlemanly manner; but all this changed when militant communism appeared on the scene.

The idea of utilizing the subservience of the French Communists to Moscow as a means of undermining the resistance of the French Army and for sabotage of war material was suggested to Abwehr Headquarters by an officer of the Training and Instruction Battalion, Special Duties, No. 800—the prototype of the Brandenburg Regiment—at a very early date. It was, however, received with much hesitant reserve; Canaris himself was, if anything, opposed to the idea, for he was too rabid an anti-communist for it to appeal to him.

Nevertheless the idea was far too good to be rejected out of hand. During the winter months of 1939/40, during which the troops on the Western front remained inactive, the Information Section of the Foreign Office drew up a number of leaflets and pamphlets designed to undermine the morale of the French Army and based, primarily, on two slogans: 'MOURIR POUR DANZIG?' and 'LES ANGLAIS SE BATTRONT JUSQU'AU DERNIER FRANÇAIS'. These slogans were blared forth on loud-speakers from the banks of the Rhine and the West Wall, and hundreds of thousands of pamphlets with the same message were distributed, some by aircraft and some addressed through the post to individuals, throughout the whole of France. The 'Die for Danzig?' leaflet was also distributed in Britain. In order that they should not be conspicuous, but should remain indistinguishable from the normal post, these leaflets were enclosed in envelopes of every conceivable size and colour, and the addresses were written by hundreds of different individuals. The task of forwarding this vast mass of paper to the country concerned was entrusted to the Abwehr and other official departments. Some were posted in Switzerland and in the then still neutral Belgium; but the major portion, already stamped with French stamps, was smuggled through by the Abwehr Belgian organization into France and there posted in the ordinary way.

The Abwehr had already made use of its liaisons with Belgian Communist Party members and functionaries for the distribution of defeatist and anti-British leaflets in France, and at the same time Communist agents had been given directives and technical instructions as regards acts of sabotage in the French war industry. Appropriate capital was made both of the common fight of Germany and the Soviet Union against the capitalist and imperialist Western Powers', and of the desertion of Thorez on October 6th, 1939. By far the most striking propaganda effect was caused, however, by Molotov's declaration of October 31st, 1939, in which he said:

'It is criminal to take any part in this war, which is a war for the destruction of National Socialism, disguised as a struggle on behalf of democracy.'

This declaration was immediately scattered in leaflet form by aircraft all over France.

To Canaris, as has already been said, the whole idea of co-operation with the Soviets was repugnant, and indeed he only tolerated it with the greatest reluctance; and as many other officers of the old Imperial era rejected it in their hearts and supported it only with the utmost hesitancy and reserve, the liaison with the Communists was maintained chiefly by two subordinate officials of the Military Intelligence Service, and for the most part on their own personal initiative and responsibility.

During the French campaign in May 1940, however, it was confirmed by the interrogation of prisoners and from other

109

sources that these subversive pamphlets had, in fact, found their way to the troops; many of the prisoners still had the leaflets in their possession and produced them in support of their claims to preferential treatment.   On the strength of this evidence, a 'Special Staff H' was formed with the task of maintaining contact with the French Communists, but with a fresh set of slogans.   These were now directed against de Gaulle who was portrayed as the mercenary tool of Western imperialism, and against the 'reactionary' British ally, who had so shamefully left the French in the lurch.   With the assistance of the Communists, touch was further established via Marseilles with the Destour Arab nationalist movement, with the object of inculcating anti-British sentiments in the French North African Colonial Army.   The latter, however, proved to be impervious to subversive influences, for it had remained completely unmoved by the catastrophe in metropolitan France, and it was only in the Navy, with its traditionally anti-British sympathies, that any success was achieved.

In occupied France, on the other hand, the Communists worked with great zeal at the distribution of subversive pamphlets launched by the German Secret Service—in many cases, admittedly, in complete ignorance of the source whence these leaflets had emanated.   Even the French press took them up.   In July 1940 the Communist newspaper *L'Humanité* wrote:

'General de Gaulle and the other minions of British high finance would dearly like to see the French fighting for the City.   But to these gentry the French reply is the *mot de Cambonne . . .*'

In March 1941 another paper, *En Avant*, wrote:

'The de Gaullists, as representatives of the city bankers, have wedded themselves to British imperialism.'

and on June 20th, 1941, forty-eight hours before Hitler's attack on the Soviet Union, *L'Humanité* declared: 'De Gaulle

110

and Catroux condone the murder of Frenchmen for the sake of the British.' Two days later the activities of Special Staff H came to an abrupt end. With the invasion of Russia on June 22nd, 1941, new orders were issued to the French Communists by the Kremlin, and these were obeyed with the same unquestioning obedience as before.

From now on the German Army of Occupation found itself face to face with a closed and united front. The Union of de Gaullists and Communists moulded the future shape of the French resistance movement, and it was a union which was destined to retain its significance for a long while after official hostilities had ceased.

On the German side, the combating of the activities of hostile intelligence services was at first in the hands of the Wehrmacht. But the longer the war lasted, the more the struggle against the resistance movement, and with it to a certain extent the fight against the enemy intelligence services, was transferred to Himmler's S.D. (the Sicherheitsdienst, the Security Service). The S.D. had a code of its own and its own particular methods, and unfortunately Supreme Headquarters, on Hitler's orders, became increasingly ruthless in its repressive measures, particularly in its attitude towards the shooting of hostages. The Abwehr was of the opinion that this shooting of hostages was not only a contravention of international law, but also that, far from achieving its object and striking terror into the hearts of the people, it would have precisely the opposite effect. While the struggle with the de Gaullists was conducted on both sides in a decent and honourable manner, the intrusion of the Communist terrorists gave it, on the French side, a totally different character. The vital and active forces of communism soon shouldered the moderate de Gaullists out of the leadership, and attacks on members of the German armed forces, depots and other military installations began to occur with increasing frequency.

The years 1942 and 1943 were remarkable for a great expansion of hostile espionage and sabotage activity. Wireless

111

operators and saboteurs were smuggled into the country in every conceivable way, and towards the end of 1943 began the systematic infiltration of organizers of resistance groups, hand in hand with Commando raids on coastal and other isolated objectives.

At the turn of the year 1941/42, one of the greatest of the enemy espionage organizations, known to the Abwehr as the Organisation Interalliée, was broken up, and many hundreds were arrested. The organization consisted of a widespread espionage net under the direction of a former Polish general staff officer with a directing staff drawn from the smaller Allied nations. It did most excellent work and was more efficient than either the British or the de Gaullist Intelligence Services.

After this blow, the activities of agents in occupied France quietened down a little for the time being, but during 1942 it increased again with renewed vigour. Preference, as before, was shown to the use of fishing smacks and the little ships of the British Navy as the means of entry and exit.

The long coastline, and especially the Breton coast, indented and broken as it is with myriads of little bays and inlets, precluded any possibility of effective supervision. Another route which found favour was that via Spain and over the Pyrenees, and here again any effective guard was very difficult. The greaetst hole of all in the German security net was, however, the line of demarcation between occupied and unoccupied France, and the Russian campaign had so reduced the strength of the occupying forces, that it was just at this very point that effective supervision was virtually non-existent. The ease with which reports could be sent across the demarcation line and the comparative immunity with which enemy agents could use their wireless transmitters in the unoccupied zone gave the other side an additional great advantage.

Finally, there was the air route. With increasing frequency reports came in of unknown aircraft flying into occupied territory, cruising over areas completely devoid of military interest, fulfilling apparently no reconnaissance mission, and certainly dropping no bombs. What they did drop was agents and containers with propaganda material, arms, munitions, explosives and directions for their use, and more and more wireless transmitters.

The German counter-intelligence organizations achieved very real successes against the enemy. But the greater the success, the more wary, of course, their opponents became. Whereas in the first half of 1942 the gatherer of information and the wireless operator were generally one and the same person, with perhaps one or two collaborators, it very soon became a case of one chief directing a whole group of agents, who for the most part were quite unknown to each other. There was therefore little point in uprooting a known enemy transmitter, if the further liaisons of its operator were not known.

To help the counter-espionage activities, wireless companies of the Wehrmacht and the Military Police were detailed, equipped with direction-finding apparatus capable of disclosing the approximate location of the enemy transmitter. Apart from the fixed direction-finding stations, there were also mobile units, disguised as ordinary civilian vehicles with civil number plates and occupied by civilians, which toured the countryside. There was also the Nahfeld apparatus, which came into operation when one of the fixed or mobile stations had confirmed the presence of an enemy transmitter. This pinpointing apparatus was particularly useful in densely populated areas, when a transmitter had been located in a particular rectangle of the town and its precise position had to be sought. Even then, intervention was extremely difficult and necessitated an intensive watch of each individual house and, in the case of many-storied buildings, of each individual floor.

The technical location of a transmitter was not by any means the final step. The work of the Abwehr, the penetration of the hostile network, had to be continued with ever greater intensity. The arrest of the enemy operator was only half the battle.

In 1942 the Germans succeeded for the first time in France

in 'turning round' an enemy wireless operator—in causing him, that is, to continue to function with his own set and in his own code, and then to send to his headquarters messages prepared for him by his new masters. In this case the opponents were the British Intelligence Service, to cross swords with whom was both worth-while and of great fascination. The maintenance of a wireless correspondence of this nature is by no means easy. The operator must not be fed exclusively with false or falsified messages, but must be given reports in which a mixture of truth and fiction is delicately blended and balanced. To continue successfully to mislead the enemy in this way demands a strong measure of centralization of control, for, obviously, if several fingers were in the pie, it would be quite impossible to carry on the game, and the plausible blend of truth and fiction would become hopelessly confused. The task was therefore undertaken by Group III D of the Abwehr Headquarters itself. Only in very special cases was some measure of de-centralization permitted; but Berlin always had to be consulted, particularly as to the handling of any specific questions asked by the enemy.

These interchanges with the British Intelligence Service lasted for varying periods, and some were maintained for quite a long time. Nor was it always necessary to 'turn' an operator 'round'; sometimes the Germans were lucky enough to capture an operator, complete with his set, call signs and code, before he had actually started to function and then they were able to establish and maintain contact using the enemy operator. For many months, for example, the British Intelligence Service was hoodwinked into believing in the existence of a resistance group which had carried out all manner of acts of sabotage, such as demolitions, train derailments, attacks on Wehrmacht personnel and the like. By making use of attacks which had actually occurred as well as of attacks which had been frustrated and by inserting untrue reports in the French press, it was possible to circumvent any check control which might have brought the game to an end.

This phantom resistance group enjoyed so great a reputation in Britain, that anything in the way of arms, explosives or other material that was asked for by wireless for its use was promptly dropped at pre-arranged places by British aircraft; and Abwehr Headquarters gradually collected a whole arsenal of arms, munitions and explosives of every kind. The Germans were particularly pleased to have got in this way a supply of plastic explosive—a dough-like substance which could be clapped on to the object to be destroyed. Then there was also a whole heap of apparently harmless objects like jam and provision tins, bottles of motor lubricating oil, especially the well-known Shell bottles; and quite apart from ordinary revolvers, the light Stenguns were very welcome. Nor did the British purveyor restrict himself to sending arms and warlike stores alone; food and luxuries were rained down, and Abwehr Headquarters soon found itself well stocked with such rarities as cigarettes and real coffee.

The arranging for these drops was always an exciting affair. The ground had to be carefully selected, the requisite light-signals placed in position, the reception committee posted ready to receive the containers and any agent who might be dropped with them. The difficulty of the task was enhanced by the fact that it had to be carried out in mufti and without the knowledge of any of the German troops who might be quartered in the vicinity; for the latter were not trained for this sort of work, and their intervention would most probably have led to a catastrophe and the rupture of the precious wireless link. Further, any agents who were dropped had to be made to believe, initially at any rate, that they really had been met by a genuine reception committee of the resistance movement.

For a time, Abwehr Headquarters had no less than five separate lines in simultaneous communication with the British Intelligence Service. In all, between April 1942 and March 1943 it succeeded in rendering innocuous over eighty enemy wireless installations, most of the operators and apparatus of which were also captured. In some cases, particularly when the opposition had taken the precaution of having several transmitters in different houses for the use of one single operator, it was able to catch only the operator or to find only his transmitter. But once it had been found out that precautions of this kind were being taken, measures were swiftly evolved to render them valueless. In March 1943 in the original occupied zone there were only six, and in the newly occupied zone some twenty enemy transmitters in action. The Abwehr activities, then, had proved to be well worth while.

These wireless connections with the enemy also put the Abwehr on the trail of that section of the Russian spy organization known as the *Rote Kapelle* which was working in France and of which I shall have more to say in the chapter dealing with Russia. At its head was one, Schulze-Boysen, a reserve lieutenant of the Air Force employed in the Air Ministry, who had also succeeded in planting some of his agents in the Abwehr itself. After repeated failures in the dropping of agents of Abwehr Section II by parachute had occurred and had been attributed to faulty technical preparation, the Air Ministry was asked to supply an officer qualified in the technique of parachuting to take charge of the preparations and execution of future enterprises. Schulze-Boysen managed to have a certain Lieutenant Gollnow detailed, who was a member of his own organization and who would have been in a position to keep him *au courant* with all Abwehr plans. Later investigation by the Gestapo failed, however, to reveal any sign that he had in fact made any such use of his opportunities. An attempt by the Gestapo to make capital out of the presence of Gollnow in Abwehr Section II met with no success, and the whole affair was confined to those members of the organization who had succeeded in installing themselves in the Air Ministry.

One section of this organization was working in France under the direction of a Russian Intelligence officer. He had succeeded in ingratiating himself with various female employees working in the offices of the Commander-in-Chief, Occupied

France. The secretary of the Chief of one of the War Administration branches, who was working in a subsidiary office of the Commander-in-Chief's office in the Chambre des Députés, afforded him invaluable assistance. She it was who introduced him to other subordinates in the Commander-in-Chief's office and to a few officers—all on a purely social basis. Not only did she deliver secret material to the Russian, but she also provided him with an official seal. The other employees and the officers concerned were guilty of nothing more serious than imprudence in having mentioned matters in ordinary social intercourse which should have been kept secret. The Russian and his principal accomplice were arrested before any serious damage was done. It then came out that the woman had been engaged without having previously been subjected to the normal security screening, and that she was the wife of a German living in Paris and had been employed for many years as a variety artist in Soviet Russia.

Some attempts, incidentally, have been made to glorify the Rote Kapelle and to give it the character of an underground resistance movement. It is quite possible that within its organization there were some perfectly sincere people who honestly believed they were supporting a purely internal organization hostile to the Nazi regime. Nothing, however, can alter the fact that the Rote Kapelle was emphatically a Russian intelligence organization, which made use of high treason on a grand scale.

The British Commando raids on the French coast from 1942 onwards imposed fresh tasks upon the Abwehr. The first enemy enterprise of any importance was a raid against a German direction-finding station—an installation which corresponded, roughly speaking, to a British radar station. The target selected was on the coast near Etretat, between Fécamp and le Havre, and was garrisoned by a few Air Force men. Under cover of darkness the British raiding party was able to land unobserved and to overpower the weak garrison, taking one prisoner.

Before nearby troops could intervene and fling the raiders back into their landing-boats, the British had ample time in which to dismantle and take with them the most important parts of the Freya and Wurzburg apparatus, which they were so anxious to obtain.

As a result of this first Commando raid, Abwehr Headquarters received orders to prepare and submit to Supreme Headquarters a precise report, not only covering the events, but also containing a comment on the security measures in force, details of any contravention of international law by the enemy and any suggestions for the improvement of defensive measures. The Abwehr, on its side, fully realized how potentially dangerous these British Commando raids could become.

But in spite of a strengthening of the coastal supervision, the raids grew in frequency and scope. From the Channel island of Sark a coastal patrol of some ten men was seized and taken prisoner. One succeeded in escaping and he reported that, contrary to international law, the prisoners had been manacled while being taken down to the landing-craft. Supreme Headquarters immediately ordered that henceforth all British prisoners were to be manacled, and from this incident there resulted a fairly long period of mutual reprisals by both sides.

An enterprise on a much greater scale was the raid on St. Nazaire. The enemy succeeded in ramming the lock-gates of the harbour with a destroyer, which was used more or less as a fire-ship—a most unwelcome success from the German point of view, as the lock was also used as a dry-dock. The actual attack was repulsed with heavy loss, and from the destroyer which had not yet sunk a copy of the complete orders for the enterprise was salved, and it was also possible to render harmless a large explosive charge, which otherwise would have caused considerable further damage.

A reconnaissance in force on a grand scale was the attempt against Dieppe, which, owing to the resistance offered by the German garrison, was repulsed with heavy losses in men and material to the enemy. An officer of the old Marine Commando of the Western campaign found a complete operation order in one of the landing-craft, and the interrogation of prisoners brought to light some extremely interesting information.

From the character of the operation and the manner in which it was executed, it became obvious that the object of the raid was not merely to cause damage and to tie down troops, but also to collect data for the preparation of an invasion and the opening of a second front in Europe.

A point always in favour of any attempted invasion was the fact that the troops in the Western occupied territories were exceptionally weak in numbers, and the anxiety of the responsible staffs can therefore be readily understood. In order to try and get a clear picture of enemy intentions, the Abwehr set about a meticulous evaluation of all the information, from agents and other sources, regarding the reconnaissance objectives of the enemy; on large-scale maps all these reconnaissance objectives, whether undertaken against places or troop distributions, were entered, with the appropriate date, and an attempt was made to draw conclusions regarding the enemy's probable invasion intentions. Towards the beginning of 1943 a distinct pattern of focal points of enemy coastal reconnaissance began to emerge. It was concentrated primarily on the vicinity of the Pas de Calais, the Seine estuary and the sector to the west of Bordeaux. Subsidiary targets appeared to be the French south coast between Sète and Marseilles and the west coast of Brittany.

To the Germans it was rather mystifying why these Commando raids should be carried out in so markedly gangster a fashion; the men taking part had blackened hands and faces and wore specially designed camouflaged clothing.

Later, a raid was carried out with little success against Port en Bessin in the Seine estuary, and another against the Casquets, in which one N.C.O. and two or three men were captured. The attack carried out in December 1942 against the German blockade runners in the Gironde estuary, on the other hand, was most successful, though in the opinion of the Abwehr it should have been prevented. A few days before it occurred two British soldiers of the Royal Marines with the usual blackened hands and faces were captured at Pointe du Grave at the extremity of the Gironde estuary. They wore a uniform well designed for this type of enterprise, with badges of rank, and when interrogated gave their rank and unit. Unfortunately, the interrogation was not conducted by Abwehr officers, or indeed by any officers qualified in any way to interrogate prisoners, and it produced no positive results; nor could any subsequent interrogation by the Abwehr be made, as the prisoners were at once shot in accordance with Hitler's 'Commando Order'.

A few days after the capture of these soldiers several blockade runners of the Europe-Japan service were sunk by plastic bombs as they lay in Bordeaux harbour. A British submarine in the Gironde estuary had launched six collapsible boats, each manned by two officers or N.C.O.s of the Royal Marines, who were then to push up the Gironde as far as Bordeaux. One boat sank soon after being launched, and its occupants swam ashore; these were the two prisoners mentioned above. The remainder passed up the long stretch of the Gironde estuary as far as Bordeaux, hiding by day in the reedy marshes of the river bank, and in this way reached and successfully attacked their targets. Some were taken prisoner, a few were killed, and the rest safely made their escape over the Spanish border; on the prisoners were found maps and instructions for the flight via Spain.

This enterprise was excellently planned; it was carried out with great dash and achieved a conspicuous success. It resulted, as may be imagined, in the introduction of measures which were of decisive importance to the work of the Abwehr in France and which were designed to draw a line of demarcation between the work of the members of the Wehrmacht and those of Himmler's organizations.

As his sphere of control had steadily expanded, Himmler had consistently pressed for the disbandment of the Secret Field Police in occupied France and the handing over of their duties and authority to the Security Police and the Security Services (the S.D.). In the summer of 1942 an order from the Fuehrer had been issued to this effect, and at the same time the whole executive power in occupied France was taken out of the hands of the military commander and placed in those of a newly created department—that of the Commander of the Security Police and Security Services in France; thus these latter two organizations found their long-cherished ambition to undertake counter-espionage work realized at last. The task of the Abwehr was rendered much more difficult in that now not only could they no longer themselves issue orders to the Secret Field Police, but also found themselves compelled to call on the Security Police and Services for assistance; and the stern repressive measures introduced by the latter merely resulted in an ever-increasing growth of the resistance movement.

The occupation of the originally unoccupied zone of France, following the Anglo-American landings in North Africa at the end of 1942, gave further impetus to the resistance movement. The German troops available for this further occupation were numerically far too weak to be able to ensure law and order in the land, and the wild country of the Massif Central, the Cevennes and the Alpine areas very quickly became havens of refuge for the resistance fighters.

The activities of the Abwehr in France did not, however, confine themselves to the combating of hostile intelligence services and to the fight against those who brought help from outside to the resistance movement. As time went on, the opportunity for the prosecution of intelligence work in other parts of the world became fewer and fewer, and the Abwehr therefore felt compelled to try and establish contacts with the outside world via the French Atlantic coast. For this, men of seafaring experience were required; among them Captain Nissen was pre-eminent. He has given the following accounts of three enterprises which he carried out:

'At the beginning of June 1940 I was called up as a pioneer

of the Instruction Regiment (Special Duty) 800, Brandenburg. Without any previous training I, still a civilian, received orders to proceed via Holland and Belgium to France, and there to seek a vessel suitable for the conveyance of agents across the Channel to England or Ireland. On the heels of the swift advance of the German armies I went as far as the Atlantic coast of France, and in the little fishing port of Cameret-sur-mer in the gulf of Brest I found a small thirty-foot yacht, built and rigged on the lines of a fishing smack. It belonged to a French colonel, the Military Attaché at the French Legation in Berne, whose wife had fled from Paris and was living on board.

'I informed the lady that I was regretfully compelled to ask her to seek other quarters ashore, as I regarded the yacht as particularly suitable for my purposes. When I reported to Abwehr II that I had found what I wanted, I was ordered to have the vessel ready for use by a certain date and to land three agents, unobserved, at any place in South Ireland which I knew to be suitable for the purpose.

'Presumably with the object of saving the vessel from confiscation by the German troops, the propeller had been removed, and as I was unable to procure a substitute in the short time at my disposal, I had to carry out my task by sail alone. As crew, late in the evening of the night I was to sail, the neighbouring Abwehr station in Brest sent aboard a completely drunken Breton fisherman, about sixty years old and found for us by a French agent. My three passengers were two young Germans born in South Africa and an Indian, who lived in Hamburg, where he worked as a ships' chandler. My duties were restricted to those of the vessel's captain, and I knew nothing whatever about their mission.

'I first set a course due west into the North Atlantic, then, turning slightly north and later east, sailed towards the south coast of Ireland. After three days' sailing I landed my passengers by dinghy under cover of darkness in the gulf of Baltimore, near the Fastnet Rock in the south-westerly extremity of Ireland. It had been my intention to sail clear of the Irish coast during the night, but owing to the fact that the wind, which till then had been blowing freshly, died down completely, I was left to drift helplessly along the coast until daylight. The vessel was camouflaged as a French fishing smack, and I had hoisted the French flag, thanks, presumably, to which two British men-of-war passed me without comment. Seven days later I arrived back safe and sound in Brest.

'That the journey had been so successfully accomplished by sail alone is due in no small measure to the fact that my old Breton fisherman turned out to be one of the finest seamen I have ever sailed with.

'In October 1940 I was ordered by Abwehr Section II to land two agents unobserved in Sligo Bay in north-west Ireland. For this enterprise I commandeered one of the famous French tunny-trawlers, the *Anni Braz Bihen* out of Douarnenez; I camouflaged the vessel suitably and made her ready for sea, and on the day fixed for sailing I was sent a crew of four Frenchmen with a Dane as engineer. Unfortunately, the four Frenchmen turned out to be completely useless as seamen, while the Dane became so sea-sick in a storm which struck us off Limerick and a hundred and fifty sea-miles west of Ireland, that he was quite incapable of serving the engines and allowed our last cylinder of compressed air, which was used to start the Diesel engine, to escape. The storm raged for five days, and it was with the greatest difficulty and under a minimum of sail that I kept the craft afloat. Without engines I was obliged to abandon my voyage and with my helpless crew I sailed back to my port of departure. The foreign crew given to me had proved completely useless, but the two German soldiers, inexperienced though they were, gave me great assistance and showed themselves to be first-class fellows in every way.

'When I reported to Abwehr II at Supreme Headquarters, I was told that, owing to the more rigorous blockade, the task of sending agents overseas in neutral vessels had become so difficult as to be almost impossible. Asked whether I saw any possibility of overcoming the difficulty, I replied that, under certain conditions, it would certainly be possible to land agents, even from the smallest of vessels, provided that they were conscientiously fitted out in a seamanlike manner and were properly equipped and manned. Provided that I were given a free hand as regards choice of vessel and selection of crew, I was prepared, I said, to undertake a mission of this nature.

'I was then given the task of finding a suitable vessel, equipping it and selecting a crew for a voyage to some port to the south of Buenos Aires in the Argentine. In the harbour of Paimpol I found an ocean-going yacht built in England, which I had known before the war and which our local naval authorities requisitioned on my behalf from the French owner. In four months I succeeded in fitting out the vessel for an uninterrupted voyage of five months' duration and collected a volunteer crew, composed of German high-seas sailors and yachtsmen, all of whom had the necessary professional qualifications and experience and promised in addition to constitute a devoted and reliable ship's company. This latter, in my opinion, was an essential pre-requisite to the successful fulfilment of the enterprise. It was, indeed, so splendid a crew, that any one of them could have taken command of the ship at least as well as myself.

'During this preparatory period I was given exact details of the project by Supreme Headquarters. We were not, after all, to go to the Argentine, but to take a Boer, one Bobby Leibrandt, and a wireless operator to South Africa. Leibrandt wanted to be put ashore on a lonely coast as near Cape Town as possible. After studying the relevant coastline, I decided to put him ashore near the Green River, about one hundred and fifty sea-miles north of Cape Town, where two rocky formations, known as "The Twins", sheltered the beach from the gigantic surf rollers common to the whole of the African coast.

'On April 1st, 1941, I reported the vessel ready for sea. On the day before we sailed, Bobby Leibrandt arrived, accompanied by the wireless operator with his very considerable amount of kit, which consisted of sabotage material and two wireless sets.

'In her papers the yacht was shown as an auxiliary warship of the German Navy under the command of myself, as a naval lieutenant. The crew, including Leibrandt and the wireless operator, were also shown as German naval ratings and provided with the appropriate pay-books.

'On April 2nd the yacht was towed out of Paimpol into the gulf of Brest by two patrol vessels of the German Navy, and on April 3rd we went to sea from Camaret-sur-mer. From the very start we struck fairly bad weather, and Leibrandt was seasick for days on end. We deliberately sailed far west into the North Atlantic before turning southwards, in order to avoid British reconnaissance aircraft as far as possible and to keep out of the way of British convoys coming from Africa to Europe. It had been agreed that in the event of being challenged at sea, we should say that we were an American yacht.

'After about ten days Leibrandt recovered from his sea-sickness and was ordered by the Captain to prepare the whole of his sabotage material for sinking by jettison, in the event of our being halted by an enemy man-of-war. This order he refused to obey on the grounds that as a Boer he did not come under the jurisdiction of the German Captain. He also refused to allow the wireless operator to accompany him ashore, because, he said, the man could not speak English and would therefore be only a source of danger to Leibrandt in South Africa.

'Off the Azores an aircraft suddenly appeared out of the clouds and bore down on the yacht. It was a British aircraft and it circled suspiciously round us, but when we waved a friendly greeting, it flew away. However, after this experience a much sharper look-out was kept, thanks to which we were able, by taking timely and evasive action, to keep out of the way of any hostile craft which cropped up on the horizon. The weather was now good, and we made excellent progress.

'On May 4th, 1941, we crossed the equator; on the 8th it was found that the main water-tank was leaking. We succeeded in effecting hasty repairs, but for which I doubt whether we should have been able to continue the voyage.

'On May 14th, at a distance of about twenty-five sea-miles, we passed the island of Trinidad, off the Brazilian coast. On May 28th we reached latitude 29° 22'—the most southerly point of the journey. The weather now became steadily worse, but the prevailing wind remained from the west and this helped us on our way to the African coast. On May 31st the ship struck a very bad south-easterly storm, which lasted for two and a half days, during which the ship was saved from grave danger only by the outstanding seamanship of the crew.

'On June 3rd we passed a steamer at a distance of about five miles, going in the opposite direction, which, however, took no notice of us. On June 7th we ran into another severe storm and were compelled to remain hove-to for several days. When the wind abated, we set course for the African coast. Cloudy skies and intermittent thick fog precluded the possibility of any absolutely accurate astronomical observation, and we continued to sail in the general direction of the coast. The next day again bad weather prevented me from fixing our position, but I continued through the night of June 8th/9th on the same course. There was a thick fog, and all preparations were made to set Leibrandt ashore. His kit was stowed into a collapsible boat and securely lashed, and we intended, if possible, to land him by night. A series of soundings showed that we were in the vicinity of the coast, but whether we had made an accurate landfall or not, we could not tell. Excitement on board was tense. The wind had died down considerably. Long before land was sighted, our noses told us that we were close inshore.

'From now on, we ran in on the motor towards the coast which lay shimmering in the bright moonlight before us. In feverish haste observations were taken, and to our delight we found that we had arrived exactly at our destination, "The Twins"—a remarkable feat of navigation on the part of Paul Temme, who, alas, was later killed. Leibrandt paddled hastily ashore. The yacht put about at once, and in a few minutes was once again lost in the thick fog which had proved such a blessing to our enterprise.

'Our mission was now accomplished, and we hoped that we should be able to get ship and crew back home again safe and unmolested. The outward voyage had lasted sixty-seven days, during which a distance of 8,111 sea-miles had been covered.

'On June 12th we passed a steamer which approached rapidly on an opposite course, but which fortunately turned out to be a Portuguese vessel. But the very next day—and, of course, it was a Friday the thirteenth—we sighted another steamer which came up so fast that we were unable to steer well clear of her by evasive action. The vessel came on straight towards us and turned out to be a British auxiliary cruiser. She signalled us to heave-to and state name and nationality. This was the most critical moment of the whole voyage, and we were more than thankful that our passenger and all his incriminating baggage were safely ashore. Although we were aboard as ratings of the Navy, we were dressed, for camouflage purposes, in any old rat-catcher civilian clothing, and there was no sign of service discipline aboard. We quietly held our course, ignoring the signals—only too well understood—which the other vessel had sent us. But our hearts admittedly sank into our boots at the unwelcome thought that we should most probably spend the rest of the war as prisoners. The enemy ship had now come within hailing distance, and we could clearly see the officers in uniform and a boat's crew, standing by ready to launch. I took a deep swig at my brandy flask and ordered the American ensign to be hoisted.

' "What ship is that?" came the hail across the water.

' "*White Star*," I replied in a typically Yankee accent.

' "Whither bound?"

' "God's own country!"

' "Are you all right?"

' "Yep, thanks, we're O.K."

'This seemed to convince the captain of the auxiliary cruiser that we really were an American yacht, and as he turned slowly back to his original course, his crew gave us a friendly farewell greeting, shouting:

127

' "Three cheers for Roosevelt!" To which we gave fervent and appropriate response, and all was well.

'There existed at the time an acute danger that the Americans might at any moment occupy the Azores; we therefore decided not to sail back to France but to make for the Spanish port of Villa Cisneros in Rio de Oro, Spanish Morocco.

'On June 22nd we reached our destination, and the voyage was over. In exactly 110 days we had sailed a distance of 14,128 sea-miles. Our ship was of thirty-four tons gross, cutter-rigged, sixty-foot, with an overall surface of 430 square feet.

'Leibrandt became a source of great annoyance to the South African authorities for several months; in co-operation with his political friends he organized a series of sabotage explosions and a very violent underground anti-British propaganda. But at last fate overtook him. He was captured, but he managed to save his neck.'

Many were the projects undertaken by the Abwehr stationed in France. In accordance with Admiral Canaris' policy of decentralization plans for these projects were drawn up and carried out by the men on the spot, who already possessed a convenient base. One example of the ramifications to which this could lead—though geographically not quite as impressive as the landing of the Boer at the Twin Rocks—was connected with the abortive vegetable oil scheme.

This was a scheme to meet Europe's deficiencies in fats by the utilization of the vegetable oils and fats of French West Africa. Partly owing to the impossibility of transporting them and partly as the result of continual fresh accumulations, vast stores were being built up, and the potential supplies from the oil-bearing crops of all kinds in these territories were so great that, if only they could be made mobile, they would more than suffice to meet the needs of the whole of Europe. Owing to British naval action, however, it was at the moment not even possible to transport enough for the requirements of North

Africa and unoccupied France. Some other way, therefore, had to be found of getting these valuable supplies to Europe.

With this object and in collaboration with the Vichy Government, it was proposed to collect and send out as many as possible of those ordinary little grinding and mincing machines, which are to be found all over France and Germany. With these, the oil-bearing fruits were to be—somewhat primitively—pressed, and a pipe-line was to be constructed for the pumping of the resultant oil to some port in North Africa.

It was anticipated that this method would give an annual yield of some 200,000 tons of oil. The support, of course, both of the Vichy Government and of the German authorities was a pre-requisite, as only through the collaboration of the two could the plan be put into execution.

As usual, the preliminary preparations gave rise to much procrastination. At last, however, agreement in principle was reached, and an expedition was sent out to survey the route to be taken by the projected pipe-line from the knee of the river Niger to the North African coast. The expedition was organized in three columns; efficient officers of the French Colonial Service, who had detailed knowledge of the terrain to be traversed, were attached to it, and it was equipped with special motor vehicles for the crossing of the desert.

The Abwehr succeeded in planting some agents among the personnel of the expedition, with instructions to report by wireless anything of military interest which came to their notice, and particularly from the left-wing column, which was marching to the east of the Niger knee and in the general direction of the Tibesti massif.

The expedition left Marseilles at the end of October 1942. But thanks to delays occasioned by bureaucratic red-tape, both French and German, it was still in Algiers when the Anglo-American forces landed on November 8th and so it all came to a premature and untimely end.

Spain presented problems of a quite different order, since it was both neutral and friendly to Germany. And here Admiral Canaris' tact and personality were of great importance and of considerable value to the Abwehr. Indeed perhaps nowhere were Canaris' high qualities of more direct service to Germany than in Spain.

The affection of Canaris for Spain and the Spaniards was both deep and sincere. It was there that he had sought refuge in the first world war, and Franco's fight against communism appealed strongly to his own implacable anti-bolshevist point of view. Whether the assistance given by Germany to Franco during the Civil War was in fact solely the result of Canaris' insistence, as has been frequently asserted in the press during recent years, may be open to doubt. But he certainly supported German intervention to the best of his ability and from the sincerest of motives.

With the Condor Legion to Spain went a fairly strong team of the Abwehr, which later, when the Civil War ended, was transformed into a War Organization and which, during the second world war, was of the greatest importance. The high repute in which Canaris was held in Spain and the bonds of friendship which bound him to Franco and to many of the generals of the Civil War days, such as Jordana, who later became Foreign Minister, and Vigon, the Chief of the General Staff, were of great value to the Intelligence Service. From Spain reconnaissance of both Britain and France was organized, and branches of the War Organization were set up in San Sebastian, Barcelona, Algeciras and Tetuan in Spanish Morocco.

The Algeciras station, which maintained a continuous watch over shipping through the Straits of Gibraltar, was also of the greatest possible value to the Navy. The fact that many hundreds of Spanish workmen daily crossed and re-crossed the frontier between La Linea and Gibraltar greatly facilitated both observation of activities in the harbour and reconnaissance against the fortress itself. Photographs of the Rock were taken periodically with telescopic-lensed cameras from a villa on the

Bay of Algeciras; in the enlargements, grouped into one composite picture, every concealed gun emplacement and every anti-aircraft battery was clearly visible. In the same way shipping movements were kept under observation by day and also by night with special night-glasses, and in co-ordination with the Estreccio Abwehr station on the African coast the sailings of Allied ships and convoys and the courses set were immediately reported to Naval Headquarters in Berlin. The British, of course, were well aware that the Abwehr was watching and frequently tried to mislead it by starting ships off into the Atlantic and then turning them round and passing them through the Straits under cover of darkness, and vice versa.

Arab demonstrations against the Allies were organized by the Abwehr from Tetuan, supported by supplementary stations in the territory of the Blue Sultan of Ifni, Rio de Oro.

Among the workmen who crossed daily to and from Gibraltar a few saboteurs were slipped across, who carried out actions of minor sabotage and, it is claimed, blew up a certain number of munition dumps. Sabotage attacks were also made on Allied shipping in the ports of Southern Spain by secreting explosive in the cases of oranges and other cargo which they were taking aboard.

At the time when Operation Felix, the attack on Gibraltar, was being planned, Canaris opened negotiations with the Alto Commissario, Beigbeder, a personal friend of his, but a man of strong pro-Ally sympathies, concerning the possibility of incorporating into the Spanish Foreign Legion a few camouflaged units of the Brandenburg Regiment. Beigbeder, however, handled the matter in a very dilatory and unenthusiastic manner —he was just on the point of setting off on a voyage to America.

Canaris took a lively interest in those Spanish units which, under the name of the Blue Division, fought on the Eastern front and did his best to see that the various difficulties which inevitably arose between the Spanish and German Services were amicably settled.

When Franco retracted from the status of a non-belligerent

to that of a full neutral in 1944, the change naturally had a very restrictive effect on the activities of the Abwehr Service in Spain; and just as Canaris was about to set out for Spain to see what he could do to save the situation, he received news from Madrid that he would no longer be allowed to cross the Spanish frontier. He then invited Martinez Campos, the Chief of the Spanish Intelligence Service, to meet him in Biarritz, but the invitation was rejected; and although War Organization Spain continued to function right up to the time of the capitulation, the real co-operation between the German and the Spanish Intelligence Services was already at an end. But by then the great days of the Abwehr, too, were nearly over.

6

The Balkans

THE activities of the Abwehr in the Balkans fall into four distinct phases. First, there was the struggle against the British and French intelligence services during 1939 and the first half of 1940. The most important aspect of this was the prevention of sabotage by the Western Allies to Rumanian oil production and Danubian transportation. With the defeat of France, British and French influence was largely eliminated from Rumania, Hungary and Bulgaria. Next came the preparations for the Greek and Yugoslav campaign. Thirdly there was the brief campaign of the spring of 1941. There followed a short period of tranquillity, soon to be broken by the ever-increasing activity of the partisans. In its fight against these latter, the Abwehr was to find itself face to face with the Soviet Intelligence.

On September 16th, 1939, the French engineer, Léon Wenger, accompanied by Captain Pierre Angot, arrived in Bucharest. His task was 'to draw up a plan for the destruction, should the necessity arise, of the oil wells, refineries, oil stocks and means of transportation, and to organize ways and means for the implementation of the plan, should it become necessary to put it into execution'. The object of the enterprise was 'as in the destructions demanded by the Allies in 1916, to deprive Germany of as much as possible and for as long as possible of the supplies of oil which she obtained from Rumania'. On September 18th, the French Ambassador, Thierry, introduced M. Wenger to the British Minister, Sir Reginald Hoare. One of the many relevant documents captured by the German Army in France goes on:

'This preliminary meeting went all the more smoothly thanks

133

to the fact that among the personnel of the British legation, as among the British engineers working in Rumania there were many individuals who, twenty years previously, had worked out with this same M. Wenger the effects of the destructions then ordered by the Allies. . . . In order to be efficacious, the envisaged destructions must, so far as possible, embrace all branches of the oil industry—production, transportation, stocks and refineries. Norton Griffith's report of January 21st, 1917, the German report on the 1916 destructions, and the findings of the Franco-British Commission of 1919/21 all show that mere improvised destruction cannot attain really efficient results.'

The above quotations have been taken from a report made by M. Wenger on October 1st, 1939; a few days earlier, on September 28th, the French Ambassador had telegraphed to his Ministry for Foreign Affairs:

'In my opinion it would be of decisive value to us to block the Danube at once and thus fundamentally to disrupt the internal waterway communications between Germany and Rumania.

'It would appear that, after a period of diminished activity attributable to the changed conditions resulting from the outbreak of war, the traffic is now expanding to hitherto unparalleled proportions. In particular, I understand that the Germans intend to transfer a portion of their Rhine fleet to the Danube, in order to make up for the deficiencies which have become apparent in the Rumanian sector.

'. . . It cannot be denied that a disruption of the Danube traffic would be an advantage to us at least equal to that which we should gain from the destruction of the oilfields themselves, for in this way the transportation of both oil and grain would be paralysed, and these two together constitute eighty per cent of Rumania's exports to Germany. The idea would be comparatively simple to realize, and I am in a position to arrange all details necessary for its implementation.'

134

On October 27th the French Foreign Minister wrote to Corbin, the French Ambassador in London:

'Our Special Services have agreed, in conjunction with the relevant British Services, to block, by means of appropriate demolitions, the passage of merchant vessels on the Danube. . . . While our own Special Services have already obtained the necessary sanction of the French Government, their British colleagues still await the acquiescence of the Foreign Office. . . . Incidentally, it was the Foreign Office which first invited the attention of our Special Services to the significance of the proposed enterprise.'

A little earlier, the Commander-in-Chief of the French Army, General Gamelin, had agreed on the desirability of the destruction of the Rumanian oilfields, and in a letter to Daladier, the War Minister, had declared:

'I suggest that the execution of the project be entrusted to M. Wenger, and I think it would be as well to give him the acting rank of colonel.'

That recollections of the destruction of the Rumanian oilfields in the first world war were still fresh in their minds and played an important part in the planning of the Allies is further proved by a remark of the French Prime Minister, Paul Reynaud, on April 27th, 1940, at a meeting of the Supreme Council held in London on the subject of the Norwegian campaign. It was decided at this meeting to give the iron-ore mines of Gellivara the same treatment that befell the Rumanian oilfields in 1916, and it was hoped that compensation for the damage could be easily agreed upon in the form of a monetary payment:

'In connection with an operation against the iron-ore mines, M. Paul Reynaud raised the question whether it would not be possible to make to the Swedish Government an offer similar to that which was made in the last war to the Rumanian Government and which led to the destruction of the Rumanian oilfields. It should be possible, he suggested, to offer the Swedish Government a fixed sum of money as compensation, should we find ourselves compelled to destroy these iron-ore mines.'

On the German side, it was of course also fully realized how important the Rumanian oilfields were to Germany's war industry, even at a time when, thanks to the treaty with Soviet Russia, Germany could count on supplies from the Baku fields —themselves, incidentally, earmarked for destruction in the Allies' programme. As early as August 1939 Admiral Canaris submitted a report on the subject to General Keitel, after his own attention had been invited by an officer of the Abwehr Foreign Section to the fact that shipping on the Danube could be brought to a complete standstill for a long time by the simple expedient of sinking a couple of barges laden with concrete at the Iron Gates in the Yugoslav sector of the river's course. Canaris assumed that the British had not forgotten the lessons of the first war and that, thanks to their good relations with Rumania, they had already arranged for this channel of communication to be closed as well as for the destruction of the oilfields themselves. The object, therefore, was to persuade the Rumanians that it would be in their own interests to protect their oil industry; the oilfields, after all, represented a very large portion of the national wealth and the protection of the lines of communication to the chief customer, Germany, was therefore most important.

The negotiations with the Rumanians were taken in hand by Admiral Canaris in person. He approached the Chief of the Rumanian Intelligence Services, Moruzow, and arranged a meeting with him, and himself personally fostered the subsequent contract. Moruzow was pro-Entente and a type of Balkan officer and official not fundamentally to Canaris' liking. But the two worked well together, and Moruzow always loyally kept every promise he made to Canaris.

The oil protection organization was set up in a number of oil firms controlled by German capital. Selected Abwehr officials were put in as supervisors and workmen, and soldiers of the Brandenburg Regiment were installed as watchmen. Linked to this nucleus was an intelligence organization which was spread over the whole of the oilfields and which was concerned with the detection of any sort of planning which might conceivably be aimed at sabotage activities. This organization worked in collaboration with Moruzow's Security Service, the *Siguranza*, and it was thanks to this collaboration that the British attempt to send explosives up the Danube from the Black Sea to the port of Giurgiu was discovered in time and frustrated.

Protection of transportation, both on the Danube and on the railways, was also organized. Soldiers of the Brandenburg Regiment dressed in mufti were posted as sentries on every goods train travelling through Hungary and on every oil-tanker on the Danube. In addition further men of the same regiment were installed in all Danubian ports as employees of the Danube Shipping Company and exercised a general supervision over all activities in these ports. The Bulgarian and Hungarian Intelligence Services were informed of what was being done, and they not only condoned the activities of the German Abwehr in their own sovereign territory, but also supported it and shielded it when necessary. The protection of transportation was expanded as the war continued to cover also the transportation of chrome ore from Turkey to Germany.

When the pro-Axis Antonescu Government assumed control in Rumania, the protection of oil transportation was carried on in open collaboration with the Siguranza and its new chief, Eugen Christescu. Moruzow was thrown into prison by Antonescu, and although Canaris interceded on his behalf, he did so in vain. Christescu was a typical Balkan Chief of Police. He had backed Germany to the hilt, but in spite of this markedly friendly attitude, he and Canaris never achieved that measure of personal friendship which characterized the relations between the Admiral and Moruzow. The latter certainly had infinitely more personality than his successor.

Co-operation with the Siguranza was now transferred from Abwehr Section II to Abwehr Section III. Secret Intelligence work in Rumania was complicated by the fact that between the Military Service and the Siguranza there existed the same

K

tension and friction as existed in Germany between the Army and the National Socialist Security Service (the S.D.) and also by the fact that there were very serious divergencies of view between Hungary and Rumania. But a measure of co-operation between Germans, Hungarians and Rumanians was, in certain directions, more than desirable, and the ironing-out of existing differences made great demands on the skill of Admiral Canaris and of his officers.

The measures taken to protect the oil and its transportation were a complete success. Canaris had assumed in August 1939, and had reported to this effect to Keitel, that the British Secret Service, which was just as familiar with the history of the first war as he was himself, and which had long ago established its organization in Rumania, would initiate sabotage acts both against the production centres of oil and against its means of transportation; why nothing of the sort was, in fact, ever attempted remains a mystery. Canaris' decision to make contact with Moruzow, who without any doubt was in close touch with the British Service, was bold, enterprising and not without a certain measure of risk. Time has proved that it was also a wise decision; and the success of his policy meant that throughout the war Rumanian oil remained at the disposal of the German armed forces.

Profiting by the experience gained there, Commandos were formed for oil protection in Rumania and smuggled over into Turkey. There they stood ready to intervene in Baku and prevent the destruction of the oilfields, if and when the German forces arrived in their vicinity.

Before Rumania entered the war, but with the tacit consent of Moruzow, an enterprise was planned against British shipping in the Black Sea. A fishing smack was sent by road from Hamburg to Regensburg and thence via the Danube to Rumania. Under a lieutenant-commander of the Abwehr and with a small German crew, its ostensible object was to fish in the Black Sea. Except, however, for one isolated attack on a small merchantman which, according to newspaper reports, sank mysteriously, nothing of any importance was accomplished.

The following report on reconnaissance activity in Greece has been drawn up by the Chief of the Hamburg Abwehr station:

'After the occupation of Denmark and Norway in the spring of 1940 and the consequent elimination of these countries as fields of Intelligence activity, I looked about Europe in an attempt to guess what fresh theatres of war might possibly come into being. The High Command, on principle, never gave the Intelligence Service any hint on the subject; but it is nevertheless the duty of an efficient intelligence officer to think ahead for himself. From the enemy point of view, security of the Mediterranean was, obviously, of vital importance, and it could therefore be safely assumed that sooner or later the German Supreme Command would turn its eyes in this direction. While making a report to Naval Headquarters, I was told, however, that there was very little likelihood of the German Intelligence Service being called upon to function in the Mediterranean, as this area was being entrusted to our Italian allies. In spite of this, I elaborated with my officers a line of thought which, in my opinion, might have considerable importance in the future.

'Our attention was focused primarily on Greece, because of its commanding position in the Eastern Mediterranean around Crete and in the approaches to the Black Sea. As a preparatory step, as early as 1940, I sent two officers to Greece, who, disguised as business men, spent several weeks in a leading Athens hotel. Their task was to gather such information as they could and to make contacts with potential agents—in fact, to lay the foundations of an organization which could be set in timely motion in the event of Greece becoming a theatre of operations. They were equipped with an A.F.U. wireless apparatus and were in daily communication from their hotel rooms with their headquarters in Hamburg. After some weeks, on completion of their preparations, they returned to Germany. When, in the spring of 1941, the situation became precarious as the result of the failure of the Italian onslaught on Albania, the German High Command decided to lighten the Italian burden by executing a southwards thrust from the Bulgaro-Rumanian area; the time had therefore come for our preparatory efforts in Greece to bear fruit. With the concurrence of Berlin, I decided to form a fully equipped Naval Commando on the lines of those Commandos formed when Denmark was invaded, to accompany the advancing troops and with orders to pass the results of their forward reconnaissance to our forces and to secure intact any installations of strategical importance.

'The Commando left Hamburg in the middle of March 1941 with its own motor transport and wireless apparatus and after a comparatively swift journey joined the troops concentrating on the Græco-Bulgarian frontier. When the invasion started, the Commando accompanied the vanguard and entered Athens with it. The army itself had great difficulty with its wireless apparatus which received such a shaking on the appallingly bad Greek roads, that they either failed altogether or only functioned intermittently. The vehicles of the Naval Commando, on the other hand, all had their own equipment, and the wireless lorries, well if somewhat primitively prepared in accordance with past experience, were so securely protected against shaking and bumping of every sort, that not on one single occasion during the advance on Athens did our wireless communication fail, and our sets were used not only for daily communication with Headquarters in Hamburg, but also by the troops for the transmission of reports of local importance.

'On entering Athens the Commander's first task was to occupy the Ministry of Marine and to secure other installations which were of importance in the further prosecution of the campaign. The comparatively young Commander accomplished his task in a most outstandingly able manner. He was so self-assured that the senior Greek Admiral surrendered the Ministry of Marine to him without further ado; and now the reconnaissance and recruitment which had been carried out many months before began to pay dividends.

'These liaisons were of great importance to subsequent operations and were of particular importance in connection with the occupation of Crete. Not a single unit of the German Navy was available on the spot to transport the troops from the Peloponnese to Crete, and recourse therefore had to be made to Greek coastal vessels. The Commander of the Naval Commando sent one of his operators, equipped, of course, with his own set, with one of these vessels. During the crossing a British cruiser suddenly bore down upon the convoy, and once more it was the Naval Commando's operator who sent the first vital reports to Command Headquarters in Athens. No Commando ever had a more efficient wireless section than this.

'At the same time as the Naval Commando was formed and sent to Greece, the Hamburg Abwehr station sent out a second Commando to the Africa Corps. Wireless operators of this Commando accompanied long-range reconnaissance flights from H.Q. Africa Corps as far as the Middle Nile and deep into the Sahara desert. In two cases aircraft were compelled to make forced landings in the desert, and their crews must inevitably have been lost, had not the Commando operator, whose set functioned independently of the aircraft's current, been able to communicate under most trying conditions with Corps H.Q. and thus arrange for a rescue plane to be sent.'

In January 1940 Admiral Canaris chanced to meet a certain staff officer in the gloomy corridors of the offices at 80 Tirpitzufer. 'I'm told,' said the Admiral, 'that you are not too happy in your present job. Is that so?'

The relations between the chief and his staff were such that the officer had no hesitation in agreeing quite frankly, explaining that he disliked the somewhat bureaucratic atmosphere at Headquarters and would far rather be employed as an Intelligence officer abroad. Asked where exactly he would choose to go, he replied that best of all he would like to be sent to Sofia.

The geographical position of Bulgaria, at the gates of the Dardanelles and flanked by the Adriatic and the Black Sea, he said, held a great fascination for him, and in Sofia, he knew, there was a vast Soviet Embassy probably largely engaged in Intelligence work. Without further ado Canaris sanctioned his transfer and told the officer to report to Sofia as quickly as possible. He gave him no further instructions as to his duties, nor did it ever enter his head to introduce him to any of the friendlily inclined Bulgarian military departments.

This casual way of initiating new activities was typical both of Canaris' method of running his Service and of the relations between himself and his officers; and equally characteristic was the manner in which the officer set about the new task entrusted to him.

Within a few days he flew to Bucharest, where he persuaded his friends to give him all the information they possessed about their Bulgarian neighbours. He assumed that, in view of the unfriendly relations between the two countries, the Rumanians would be able to supply him with far better and more precise information about the country he was about to visit than could be obtained from any reports filed away in Berlin; and so it proved. He then took the Balkan Express to Giurgiu, the Danubian port on the Rumanian side, and thence, via Rousse on the Bulgarian bank he proceeded to Sofia. After a stay of a week or so, during which he made no contact whatever with any official department, he returned to Berlin, reported his impressions to his chief and outlined his ideas on how he proposed to set up shop in Bulgaria. In order to be able to function as a liaison officer of Abwehr Headquarters he was appointed Adviser on Military Economic Affairs to the Military Attaché at the German Legation in Sofia—in a purely civilian capacity.

He reported for duty in March 1940 and was given a small room at the Legation as his office. During his first year, entirely on his own and without any personnel, he quietly acquired a thorough grasp of Bulgarian affairs and a sound knowledge of the Bulgarian mentality; in an unobtrusive manner he succeeded in making contacts with, and giving instruction to, individuals who might be of use in any potential Intelligence work in the future. The success of this first year's work, which brought a rich harvest of information about Germany's present and future enemies, is attributable above all else to the fact that this 'one-man-band' was able to work in complete obscurity. The less publicity he got, the better he was pleased!

He scrupulously obeyed the instructions of his chief to respect the position in which Bulgaria, a neutral State, found herself *vis-à-vis* Germany's active enemies, and his activities as liaison officer to the Royal Bulgarian General Staff were reduced to the lowest possible minimum.

But as the crisis in the south-eastern sector became more acute, the camouflage of this station gradually wore thin. A few assistants, among them an independent wireless section for direct communication with Berlin Abwehr Headquarters, were sent out. The other home Abwehr stations whose activities were directed towards the south-east—and many who had nothing whatsoever to do with that part of the world—sent 'special agents' in increasing numbers via Bulgaria into the remoter sections of the Near East, Turkey and the like. Being completely ignorant of the countries in which they found themselves, these agents invariably formed what were called 'Levantine liaisons' and caused a variety of notorious and noisy incidents. 'Levantine liaisons' was an Abwehr expression: it meant dealings with a certain species of Balkan amateur spy who, getting wind of an Axis organization in his vicinity, was only too eager to offer his services for spot cash or for some other profitable transaction—but always to his own exclusive advantage. Gradually, however, the Abwehr succeeded in ridding itself of this disreputable riff-raff.

During the first quarter of 1941 a number of camouflaged military staffs were quietly slipping into a friendly Bulgaria, and making the technical preparations for the advance of German troops from Rumania through Bulgaria for the invasion of Greece and Yugoslavia. All these staffs made contact with the posts which had meanwhile been set up by the KO. (War Organization) and took advice as to the attitude they should adopt in the country. As it was of particular and urgent importance that relations between German troops and the Bulgarian population should be friendly and undisturbed, a small handbook on behaviour in a friendly country was drawn up, with the co-operation of the War Organization, for the guidance of the troops when they arrived.

Some two weeks before the opening of hostilities with Greece and Yugoslavia, the War Organization was called upon to make preparations, in collaboration with the appropriate branches of the Bulgarian Army, for the intervention of units of Abwehr Section II (Brandenburg Regiment), which were to be entrusted with the so-called 'material protection' of the entire lines of communication behind the German operations, from the Danube right up to the Greek and Yugoslav frontiers. The task of these units was to protect vital installations such as power-houses, level-crossings, bridges and the like against anticipated sabotage attacks by Anglo-American agents or by the communist underground. They were also to provide scouts posted on the Greek and Yugoslav frontiers who were to act as guides and interpreters for the first waves of the German invasion. Finally, the War Organization, with the concurrence of the Bulgarian authorities, was to mobilize all surplus motor transport, which would be valued and purchased by a Special Commission of the War Organization, and would be available to facilitate the swift transit of the German units and of the Special Duty Commandos. These preliminary tasks were so swiftly and efficiently carried out, that when the German troops marched in, scouts, guides, interpreters and mechanical transport were all available in ample measure, and the whole operation was executed without a hitch of any kind.

An interesting feature of the operation was the arrival and onward transportation of the 'material protection' units of the Brandenburg Regiment, which landed out of the low-lying clouds into the mists of an early April morning at the Sofia airport and were then driven straight away to the scenes of their activities in motor transport provided for the purpose. The whole business was completed between five and nine o'clock in the morning. The units were first taken to Bulgarian barracks, where, as had been arranged, they were received by waiting German interpreters; some units there changed into Bulgarian uniforms, and the whole force was then directed, under the ægis of the Bulgarian military authorities, to the various installations it was to guard.

Later, friendly Bulgarian officers told with broad grins how comical these 'Bulgarians' with a strong Bavarian accent looked in the villages near the frontier, and what a hearty welcome these German soldiers were given in the little homesteads of the Bulgarian peasantry.

So dawned the day on which the Twelfth Army, ready and waiting, under Field-Marshal List, was to throw its bridges like lightning across the broad Danube and begin its swift march through Bulgaria. No orders or appeals by the Bulgarian authorities were required to ensure a friendly welcome for the brothers-in-arms of 1914/18 from every Bulgar, whether in the big towns or in the tiniest of Balkan hamlets. Everywhere men, women and children stood from morn till night on the thresholds of their homes, giving hearty cheers for the 'Germanskis' and offering them bread and salt, the tokens of friendship and hospitality. These poor people offered everything their modest homes and hearths had to give to the Germans in a sincere and heart-warming brotherhood, which could have found no more touching mode of expression; and to the credit of the German soldiers it must be said that in their acceptance of all this hospitality they behaved in an exemplary and most praiseworthy manner. In an army which, after all, was of very considerable size, not one single case of improper behaviour came to light.

After the turmoil of these operations had died away in Bulgaria and the hostile territories of Yugoslavia and Greece had been occupied, the radius of action of the War Organization was expanded to include the Grecian province of Thrace and the liberated Dobruja. Then, in consultation with the neighbouring intelligence stations and on orders from Abwehr headquarters in Berlin, the whole War Organization was remodelled in a form comparable to that of an Abwehr station in Germany itself, and subsidiary stations were set up on the Danube, on the Black Sea opposite Turkish territory, in Thrace and in that portion of Serbian Macedonia which was ceded to Bulgaria.

A widespread internal wireless network joined all these out-stations and subsidiary posts with Headquarters in Sofia, replacing the very inadequate Bulgarian means of communication and travel and guaranteeing a swift and secure channel for the exchange of appreciations and the transmission of reports. In the weeks following the conclusion of the campaigns the War Organization had increased to a strength of nearly two hundred and fifty and had become a regular Abwehr station, with its own wireless communication system, its own cipher section, its technical and photographic sections and its advisers on secret inks, their manufacture, use and methods of detection.

Throughout the second world war, no state of war existed between Bulgaria and Soviet Russia; on the contrary, their relations were marked by a friendship which had originated in the traditional gratitude of the Bulgars for Russian help in liberating them from the Turkish yoke and which, on the Bulgarian side, was undoubtedly sincere. Nevertheless the Soviet Embassy and its consulate in Varna on the Black Sea were used throughout the war, and particularly after the opening of hostilities between the German Reich and the Soviet Union, as an intelligence station of the greatest importance for the whole of the Balkan area. Any penetration into the heart of these Missions was quite impossible, since the Bulgarian Government, for obvious political reasons, zealously protected the extra-territoriality of these Russian representatives.

The members of the Soviet Missions were under the constant and powerful protection of the Bulgarian police, and thanks to this immunity the Russians were able to direct an active and militant underground movement served by a vast number of agents recruited throughout Bulgaria and Macedonia from among the opponents, Bulgars and others, of the Hitler regime. In order to make what follows intelligible, it must be mentioned that Sofia was somewhat ironically described as 'the greatest naval base in the South-east', although, in fact, the city lies some hundreds of miles from the sea. It earned this title because the Naval Command South had been in residence there since 1941. This headquarters consisted of several hundreds of officers, officials and subordinate personnel and occupied a vast number of apartments in the Bulgarian capital; while outside the gates of the city, just beyond the beautiful Boris Park, was a camp inhabited by many thousands of naval ratings, who were earmarked for action in the Ægean and Black Seas, on the coasts of which further naval stations had been established. This organization was on very friendly and cordial terms with the civilian population of Sofia and its environs, and in the evening the German tars could be seen, before Retreat, streaming through the Boris Park back to their camp and feeling obviously as much at home as if they were in some German garrison town.

Reports regarding the activities of the militant underground movement flowed in a steady stream into the War Organization, with the result that the German staffs and units stationed in Bulgaria were constantly kept informed of any danger which might be threatening. But the deceptive peace which reigned as the outcome of German-Bulgarian friendship lulled the troops into a state of security and blunted their alertness to the growing dangers, until one day, towards the end of 1942, two naval ratings on their way back to camp were shot down by unknown assailants in the Boris Park. The echoes of these shots shocked public opinion and galvanized the excellent Bulgarian police, rousing them from their placid day-to-day routine. Police Headquarters immediately took drastic security measures, which included a complete sealing-off of the capital from the outside world and a house-to-house search of all

147

potential hide-outs for undocumented and unauthorized residents. These measures brought to light a considerable number of Red underground fighters, who stated that they had for the most part been transported across the Black Sea by submarine for subversive activities in Bulgaria. Others had slipped in via Rumania and Yugoslavia, to act as instructors and individual saboteurs. Subsequent interrogations confirmed, and indeed greatly added to, the information already collected by the War Organization.

As a net result the War Organization set up a special service with the task of investigating, collating and reporting to W. O. Headquarters every act of sabotage, however insignificant, and every attack, either on military personnel or on civilians, throughout the whole of the Bulgarian territories. By this means it was hoped swiftly to obtain a comprehensive picture of the gradually expanding field of activity and the growing strength of the underground movement. On this would be based the counter-measures necessary to combat them.

The Boris Park murders were finally cleared up by the War Organization and the Bulgarian police working in unison. Three civilians, speaking a broad Hamburg dialect and in possession of papers identifying them as members of the Todt Organization, had, apparently, for some considerable time been on friendly terms with the German naval lads, from whom bit by bit they obtained details of the German staffs and troops resident in and around Sofia. Thanks to a precise personal description of the presumed O.T. members and to a photograph taken by a German sailor on some festive occasion, the three civilians were finally identified as members of the Hamburg Communist Party of the 1920s, who had fled to Soviet Russia via Copenhagen in 1932. There, as was later established, they had received a thorough training as saboteurs, specializing in attacks on merchantmen and men-of-war. When the underground struggle in the South-east increased in intensity, they were landed by submarine for the purpose of carrying out acts of sabotage and violence. Among the latter were to be included assassination of members of the German garrison, with the object of disturbing the good relations existing between the Germans and the Bulgarian authorities and population. These attempts increased consistently throughout 1943; they were directed not only against members of the German armed forces, but also, increasingly and particularly in Macedonia, against prominent national personalities like General Lukov, mayors and members of the Communal Council and Administration, and against anyone, in general, who was pro-German or of royalist sympathies.

Eventually a scrutiny of Bulgarian territory, undertaken district by district, showed an ever-increasing number of acts of sabotage executed by the Red underground movement; and these, taken in conjunction with the reconnaissance results obtained by the War Organization Sections I and III F, enabled the Abwehr to get a clear idea both of the concentrations of hostile underground forces and of their respective spheres of activity. In country districts the dangers and hazards increased to a truly alarming degree; very soon it became unwise to traverse the long stretch of lonely mountain country into Thrace without an armed escort, to wander anywhere alone in the Balkan mountains or even to move alone about the countryside in the vicinity of Skoplje. An ever-tightening wireless network, working in co-operation with War Organization patrols, admittedly did something towards restricting the unfettered and unobserved activity of the underground movement, but the measures introduced by the Bulgarian authorities were far too clumsy and unmethodical to have any chance of success against extremely mobile opponents, acquainted with every inch of the country in which they were operating.

As a result of this state of affairs, the War Organization evolved a plan, at first purely theoretical, for the employment of Anti-Partisan Platoons (A.P.T.s). These were to be formed of groups of young local inhabitants, well acquainted with the countryside and physically and ideologically pre-eminently suitable for the difficult task of anti-guerrilla warfare, with a small but solid nucleus of regular German troops equipped with a wireless section. At first two experimental platoons of this nature were raised, trained and armed with light automatic weapons which were then in very short supply, and which sometimes had to be obtained by the most devious and dubious methods. The prime essential was to imbue the platoons with an *esprit de corps* of absolute comradeship and unconditional loyalty. They were then allotted definite operational areas, within which they could move at will, and with the single and explicit order that they were to use any and every means, regardless of cost, to gain the upper hand over the hostile bands of partisans in their area. Here, obviously, was a case where the principle that 'a reign of terror can be broken only by counter-terror' had to be followed to the hilt, and while the cumbersome efforts of regular Bulgarian divisions and regiments failed consistently and completely in all their attempts to comb the all but impassable mountain districts, these special platoons achieved considerable success. Mobile and swift-moving, adopting as their own the tactics employed by the Partisans, the A.P.T.s became the only weapon which the opponents had really good cause to fear.

The suggestion of the War Organization that the whole of Bulgarian territory should be divided into operational areas and handed over to A.P.T.s was, unfortunately, not put into practice. Rather, a course was adopted by the Bulgarian Government, which gave the Partisans an advantage of which they could never again be robbed and enabled them to gain complete mastery over the whole length and breadth of Bulgaria. Towards the end of 1943 the Bulgarian Government decided to raise a Corps of Gendarmerie—a body which had never before existed in the country—and to entrust to it the suppression of the Partisans. To form it, the very excellent Bulgarian police was robbed of nearly fifty per cent of its best men. They were detailed to their new duties with bewildering speed, in spite of the fact that neither the Bulgarian State nor its ally, the German Reich, was in a position adequately to provide the armament, weapons, barracks, transport, wireless equipment and all the rest which were essential to the fighting efficiency of a special force of this nature. As a result the Corps of Gendarmerie, as originally envisaged, simply never came into existence, and the Red enemy was consequently able to take advantage of this dangerous vacuum to gain complete and undisputed supremacy throughout the land. Here, clearly and beyond doubt, was a gross contravention of every accepted operational and tactical principle and of every accepted rule for the maintenance of law and order. With the bombing of Sofia and other towns from January 1944 onwards, the pace of internal lawlessness, rebellion and disruption began to accelerate till it culminated in complete collapse in the face of the swiftly approaching Russian front in September 1944.

With the successful termination of the short Balkan campaign in 1941, the German High Command thought that it had freed itself from any further need for preoccupation with that part of Europe. This proved to be a faulty conclusion, for as in Bulgaria, so in the other almost inaccessible mountain fastnesses there developed a resistance movement which it was not possible to overcome. In Yugoslavia this movement assumed such massive proportions that large military forces had to be employed against it. Among them were various units of the Brandenburg Division, from the war experiences of which the following report is taken.

At the end of April 1943 the 4th Brandenburg Regiment was transferred to the Kossove-Mitrovitza (Amselfeld) district and, prior to being switched to take part in an encircling movement against Tito, it was ordered to find out the whereabouts of the Chetnik leader, Draga Mihailovic, and to capture him. As reinforcements a company of Albanians was raised; and it was also found that the armed Montenegrin miners were ready in large numbers to enlist in the German forces and to take part in the war against Tito.

At the beginning of 1943 Tito felt that he had been left in the lurch by the Russians, help from the West was all too slow in arriving, and the Klagenfurt Abwehr station decided that the time had come to establish direct contact with him. This was successfully done, and at a subsequent conference between a German and Tito's representative, the latter declared that Tito was prepared to cease hostilities against the Germans, provided that, under supreme German sovereignty, he was given control of the whole of Yugoslavia, including Croatia. This, however, was a proposal which was foredoomed to rejection, primarily because Croatia was already the subject of an agreement with Italy, and also because the Armed Forces Supreme Command (the O.K.W.), which was responsible for operations in the Balkan theatre of war, was of the opinion that Tito could be eliminated within a very few months.

Before the drive against Tito started, the 4th Brandenburg Regiment had found out that Mihailovic was receiving support both from Great Britain and from Italy. The Italian garrison troops held the towns and the partially fortified camps, but left the remainder of the country to General Mihailovic's Chetnik organization, and, in return for services rendered, gave them food, arms and protection. Mihailovic himself lived in Kolashin in Montenegro, where he had a reliable personal body-guard of a few thousand men, and whence he maintained the closest contact with the Italian Commanding General in Pod-goritz (Titograd).

It was at the beginning of May 1943 that the commandant of the 4th Brandenburg Regiment discovered Mihailovic's where-abouts. Although his orders were to capture him, he went, accompanied by only two interpreters, to Kolashin, where he found Mihailovic's two Chiefs of Staff and was taken by them to the General himself. Mihailovic claimed that he had a royalist partisan following, particularly in old Serbia, which amounted to several hundred thousand men. So far, he said, he had forbidden any hostilities against German troops. His arch-enemy was Tito, and he made Germany the offer that she should immediately march, together with his partisans under

152

the Italian leadership against their prime mutual enemy, the Communists. He further proposed, as a proof of the earnestness of his intentions, and, to a certain degree, as a guarantee against the defection of his troops, to raise a Yugoslav division to fight for Germany on the Eastern front. In return he demanded recognition of himself as Minister for War in Serbia which was to be reconstituted as a sovereign state, and the continued support of the Chetnik movement by the German Government and the German Wehrmacht. A limiting factor to such an agreement, he added, was the fact that it could be operative only until such a time as American or British forces landed on the Dalmatian coast; if and when that occurred, he said, he felt that he would no longer be able to vouch for the reliability of his troops. Meanwhile, he was prepared to launch an appeal to the Yugoslav people over the Belgrade radio.

Mihailovic's intentions were quickly to be put to the test, for at that very moment Tito launched his attack from the north against Montenegro, and the communist danger became both pressing and apparent. Supreme Headquarters, however, rejected Mihailovic's proposals, the Commandant of the 4th Brandenburg Regiment who had conducted the negotiations was removed temporarily from his command, and Mihailovic's two Chiefs of Staff, Dyuresec and Pugovic, in contravention of a solemn undertaking, were arrested by the Nazi Party Security Service and taken out of the country.

In the middle of May 1943, although the fact was not known in Germany, the 1st Mountain Division and an Italian Army Corps were face to face and on the point of opening fire for ten whole days. Had Mihailovic's offer been accepted, the chief burden of the fight against Tito would have been transferred to the Germans, and it is more than probable that the Tito forces would have been completely annihilated. As it was, the arrest of Mihailovic's Chiefs of Staff and the breaking off of negotiations with Mihailovic himself were followed by the disarmament of the Serbian and Montenegrin mountaineers, carried out for

153

the most part by the S.S. Prinz Eugen Division with the utmost brutality; and although admittedly this led to the disintegration of Mihailovic's Chetnik movement, it also made a present, at a decisive moment, of tens of thousands of partisans to Tito.

7

Soviet Russia

THE Russian campaign was so vast and, compared with the other campaigns of the second world war, of such long duration, that it is impossible to give a full picture of the Abwehr activities which it entailed. However, the following incidents should provide a fairly comprehensive picture of the problems which confronted the German Intelligence Service on the Eastern front and of how they were dealt with.

Intelligence work against Soviet Russia was rendered very difficult, if only because of the lack of any common land frontier; apart from this, however, was the fact that all commercial relations with foreign countries were conducted on the Russian side exclusively by government departments, with the result that there was very little travelling either from or to the outside world, and it was therefore all but impossible to send itinerant agents into the Soviet Union. German business men had the entrée into certain portions of the Union during the 1920s, when the Russians were still making commercial concessions and were employing German assistance in the reconstruction of their industry and agriculture. But these business men, with very few exceptions, refused on principle to cooperate in any way with the Intelligence Service.

Reconnaissance of the Russian Army by the Abwehr was not, in the 1920s, of the same importance to the Wehrmacht as was that of the Polish Army. The Soviet Union was far from being regarded as a potential enemy; on the contrary, friendly relations and a mutual exchange of information were then the order of the day. The heavy weapons, which were denied to Germany under the terms of the Versailles Treaty, could readily be manufactured in Russia, and as the Germans, from experience gained in the first war, contributed not a little to the manufacture and perfection of these weapons, they were fairly well informed about the modern armament of the Russian land and air forces and about the strength and composition of the Russian Army. As regards the Navy, the Intelligence Service by meticulous attention to details succeeded in gaining a fairly comprehensive picture of the Russian Fleet and its bases. However, I do not believe that there was any large-scale penetration by German agents of the Red Army and the Red Fleet as was alleged during the trial of Marshal Tukachevsky and other leaders of the Soviet forces during the great purge of the middle 'thirties. Though not myself in the Abwehr at that time, I am satisfied that the fantastic charges of treason advanced by the Russian public prosecutors were baseless.

Just how difficult it was to make an intelligence survey of Russia was brought home to the Germans by a study of the files of the Polish Intelligence Service which fell into German hands at the end of the campaign in Poland. Although Poland had a long common land frontier with the Soviet Union, the information gathered by the Poles was not, in essentials, any more comprehensive than that possessed by the Germans.

But as soon as the German and Russian forces found themselves face to face on the conclusion of the Polish campaign, reconnaissance of the Russian Army was at once taken in hand by German agents and by many former Polish agents now working for the Abwehr; and when war with Russia broke out in June 1941, the distribution, arms and armament of the Russian force and the location of their aerodromes, at least in that portion of Poland which they occupied, were known with comparative exactness.

This feat of the Intelligence Service was all the more remarkable in that the Russians did their utmost to prevent any penetration of the Soviet occupied territory. Wherever a dry boundary existed, they immediately constructed a barrier. In front would be a barbed wire apron; behind it a strip some ten or fifteen yards wide was cleared, ploughed up and raked over in such a manner that any footprints on it would be immediately apparent. Listening posts were constructed at regular intervals, and the wire apron itself was dotted along its whole length with a variety of alarm signals, most of them, admittedly, of a somewhat primitive nature. Behind this barrier was a security belt, some twenty miles in breadth. A certain portion of this frontier area was cleared of all inhabitants, and in the remainder the inhabitants were forbidden to give shelter to strangers.

The outfitting of agents made great demands on the forward Abwehr out-stations. For employment as agents only those could be considered, of course, who had a complete command of the language and whose appearance was in no way suspicious. They had to be fitted out with appropriate clothing, and this did not end with externals; underclothing, shoes, matches, cigarettes and tobacco, all of the right kind, had to be provided, and even a single button which seemed to be of western origin, could become a source of very great danger. The hardest task of all, however, was the provision of documents. It was not merely a question of providing the necessary personal identification papers; each agent had to be equipped with passes which proved both his right to be in any particular district which he happened to be traversing and his authority to enter the district for which he was eventually making.

Before the beginning of the campaign in June 1941, the Abwehr had identified seventy-seven Russian infantry divisions on Polish territory—a total which the Foreign Armies Section of the Army General Staff queried at the time, but one which subsequently proved to be correct.

For the Russian campaign the organization originally set up by the Abwehr for previous campaigns was enlarged, and one or more Reconnaissance Commandos were attached to each Army Group.

Apart from the Abwehr stations set up to penetrate into Russian territory itself, there was one other source of information—the Russian émigré colony, the innumerable Russian officers and civilians who had streamed westwards after the revolution. The majority had settled in France, but during the 1920s and 1930s there were also many Russians in Berlin who had with difficulty adapted themselves to the German way of life and painstakingly fitted themselves into the German economy. Many of the ex-officers had no knowledge of anything except what their military careers had taught them; nevertheless a few among them had succeeded in remaining in touch with people in their own country, and every now and then the Abwehr obtained a little material which was of interest from the Intelligence point of view; most of what was received, however, was false and more likely to lead to confusion than to be of any value.

But among these émigrés there were a few important contacts which went back to the days of the first war. On the outbreak of the Russian revolution Germany had given lively support to the attempts being made to set up an independent Ukrainian State and had agreed to the nomination of the Hetman Skoropatski as Head of the Government, a man whose ideas leaned towards the creation of an autonomous Ukrainian State within the framework of a Czarist Greater Russia. But by the 1920s it had become obvious that this could never be achieved, and when, round about 1937, the Abwehr began to consider whether some co-operation with the Ukraine would not be worth while, Skoropatski and his followers were not taken into consideration; it was decided, rather, to cultivate a co-operation with the O.U.N. (the Organization of Ukrainian Nationalists), the leader of whom was one Konovalec, for whom Admiral Canaris had a marked personal predilection. Although Canaris himself was a dyed-in-the-wool conservative and monarchist, he nevertheless preferred the revolutionary Konovalec to the aristocratic Skoropatski. Co-operation with Konovalec, however, was not destined to last for very long. Shortly after the preliminary conferences he was murdered, while still in exile in Holland.

The leadership of the organization was then taken over by Melnyk and his chief supporter, Ricco Jary, an ex-Imperial

158

regular officer. Melnyk was the estate agent of the Greek Orthodox Metropolitan of Lemberg, a Count Szeptyski, himself an ex-officer of the Imperial Russian Army, an aged and most venerable figure, who was 'the uncrowned King' of the Galician Ukrainians. After the Polish campaign the Abwehr station in Cracow got in touch with Stepan Bandera, a radical Ukrainian nationalist revolutionary, who had a considerable following, particularly among the younger elements, in the Galician Ukraine. Unfortunately there were grave divergencies of view between Melnyk and Bandera, for the former, with his more constitutional reform aspirations, rejected sharply the latter's violent and radically revolutionary opinions. After a while there occurred a split between the two, which became wider with the formation of the Vlassov units, whose sympathies leaned emphatically towards a Greater Russian policy. The O.U.N. was financed for the most part by Ukrainians who had migrated to the United States and had there formed themselves into national associations.

In 1938 the Abwehr began the military training of young Ukrainians in an unobtrusive and isolated holiday camp on Lake Chiemsee. Primary emphasis was laid on the training of junior leaders for guerrilla warfare, and some groups were sent to Abwehr Section II's laboratories in Tegel near Berlin and to the training establishment at Quenzgut for instruction in the use of explosives and other subjects appropriate to the execution of sabotage attacks. The Japanese were particularly interested in these attempts by the Abwehr to make use of the Ukrainian and other Eastern minorities. Quite a number of Russian emigrants, predominantly Ukrainians, had settled in Manchuria and had there sought to collaborate with the Japanese.

The atmosphere of mutual trust and confidence created by this co-operation between Germans and Ukrainians was put to a severe test at the time of the solution of the Carpatho-Ukrainian problem in 1939. Considerable dissatisfaction had already been aroused by the Vienna Arbitration Award of 1938, which decided between the rival Polish and Ukrainian claims in the Carpatho-Ukrainian territories. When Hitler decided in 1939 to hand over this territory to Hungary, disappointment and consternation became rife among members of the O.U.N. Bands of Carpatho-Ukrainians offered armed resistance to the incoming Hungarians and suffered heavy casualties, while many more were captured and flung into Hungarian prisons. It was Canaris who succeeded in having them transferred to Germany, where the Abwehr assumed responsibility for their future welfare.

The General Staff was at this time most anxious to undermine the loyalty of the Ukrainians serving in the Polish Army. It was thought that the appearance, on the German side, of a Ukrainian Volunteer Corps would lead to desertions by Ukrainians from the Polish Army. The Ukrainian groups which had been trained by the Abwehr were sent to an isolated sector of the Dachsteingebirge in East Slovakia, whence they were to advance, when the campaign opened, into the Galician sector and then swiftly infiltrate behind the Polish front into East Galicia, with the object of rousing their compatriots to guerrilla warfare against the lines of communication of the Polish forces. It was anticipated that this move would be of more value politically and for propaganda purposes than in the purely practical military sense—an appreciation, incidentally, which applies to every enterprise of a similar nature.

But all these preparations were once more rendered abortive by a change of policy. Hitler and Ribbentrop decided to leave East Galicia to the Russians, and the Abwehr therefore had no option but to withdraw the more compromised among the Ukrainians from the territory east of the San; at the same time, at the request of the Greek orthodox clergy, the most valuable possessions of the churches in Przemysl were removed to the west bank of the San by an Abwehr Commando shortly before the arrival of the Russian vanguard.

At the end of September 1939 the Russo-German Treaty of Friendship was signed, and the Abwehr was then forbidden to have anything more to do with the O.U.N. or to support it financially or in any other way. At this point the Japanese stepped in and saved the situation. As signatories of the German-Japanese Anti-Comintern Pact of 1936, they were utterly dismayed at the latest turn taken in Russo-German relations. They were in close touch with White Russian émigrés in Germany, who were very helpful to them in the production of anti-communist propaganda and who had transformed a villa on one of the Berlin lakes into a secret printing establishment. Through one of the officers in their Embassy, the Japanese at once got in touch with the Ukrainians who had been working with Abwehr Section II, took over the maintenance of contact with the O.U.N. and—though not much was ever said about it—they kept up the liaison and looked after the Ukrainians until June 1941. Then of course everything was once more quite different, and the Germans were most anxious to resume control of the Ukrainian contacts which they had let slip.

While Abwehr Section II in Berlin was responsible for the technical arrangements and the material equipping of all enterprises aimed at objectives deep within the enemy country, the so-called 'Front Duties'—Intelligence duties, that is, at the front itself and in the immediate support areas—were directed by the Army Group or Army concerned. For the execution of these duties the Abwehr Commandos (I, II and III) were placed under the command of the IC.s, the General Staff Officers at Army Group or Army, as the case might be, who were responsible for Intelligence work at the front; and when required, units of the Brandenburg Division were also similarly attached.

Abwehr Headquarters was solely responsible for the personnel and equipment of these attached Commandos. This dual control—with Berlin running the technical side and the commander-in-chief on the spot giving the tactical orders—was not a very happy solution, and there were endless complications, similar to those which arose from the dual control of the armed S.S. formations and the Security Service Shock Troops, exercised on the one hand by Himmler and on the

161

other by the commander-in-chief in whose area the units were operating.

Direct liaison with the General Staff was maintained by the 'Abwehr Command Staff WALLI', which was stationed at Nikolaiken in East Prussia, in close local touch, that is, with 'WOLFSCHANZE' (Hitler's Headquarters) and 'ANNA' (Head-quarters, Army General Staff).

Even when the war of movement had crystallized on the Eastern front into static warfare, gaps and thinly held areas were to be found in nearly every sector of the German and Allied fronts through which it was possible to slip agents; and where this was not possible, or where it was desired to operate deeper in the enemy back areas, parachutists were used, of whom the Abwehr had a Special Wing, recruited in part direct from the civilian population.

Most of all, however, prisoners-of-war were used as agents. Many of the Abwehr Commandos, seizing the opportunity when there was a lull on their front, had set up a small training camp and ordnance store, where agents and saboteurs could be instructed and equipped for their missions; and in view of the enormous distances on the Eastern front, this decentralization of front-line Abwehr activity was essential and proved to be invaluable.

It was generally and unanimously agreed that in the use of prisoners as agents a 'strike-while-the-iron's-hot' technique offered much the greatest promise of success; the sooner the agents could be sent off on their mission after receiving the necessary training and instruction the better. If any long period was allowed to elapse between the issue of instructions and the going into action, the agents, it was found, often turned 'sour' —and then they generally failed. Apart from this, a long wait behind the German front line gave them, unavoidably, the opportunity of acquiring a knowledge of German methods and personnel and of the identity of fellow-agents which, if they were harbouring any intentions of double-crossing, might be very dangerous. In any case the issue of instructions to a number of agents at one and the same time is always hazardous; but nearly all secret services are guilty of disobedience of this principle, particularly in wartime, partly through lack of personnel, pressure of time or for some other reason caused by war conditions, but also, sometimes, just to save themselves trouble. The same general principle applies also to the 'standard equipment' of agents. Again and again the station of origin has been recognized by the watch or the camera or the matches provided out of the 'quartermaster's store'.

That these operations were not expanded into acts of sabotage of tactical or strategical significance, or even into a nuisance value on a big scale, is attributable partly to professional short-comings in the Abwehr, but principally to the unhappy policy pursued by Germany in the Eastern territories and the treat-ment meted out to minorities within the Soviet Union.

Of the many operations carried out by the 'Brandenburgers' during the Russian campaign, the following small selection must here suffice.

During the advance of Army Group North into Latvia in the summer of 1941, a detachment of the Brandenburg Regi-ment seized the bridge over the Dvina and saved it from destruction. The men, disguised as Russian wounded, drove on to the bridge with the Russian rearguard and then by a surprise attack gained possession of it. Thanks to this opera-tion the advance of Army Group North on Riga was main-tained without any loss of time—a success which the Com-mander-in-Chief, Field-Marshal von Leeb, gratefully acknow-ledged in a letter to Admiral Canaris.

But such attempts to mislead the enemy did not always go so smoothly. On one occasion during the advance in the Caucasus, it was desired that the destruction of a certain dam by Soviet engineers be prevented. The leading German lorry had already been cleared by the Commissar in control and its passengers, in the guise of utterly exhausted stragglers from the Russian rearguards, were about to clamber back into it, when the Commissar spoke to a 'comrade' sitting idly by the road-

163

side. As bad luck would have it, this was an N.C.O. from Hamburg, who did not speak a word of Russian. Lieutenant Baron Foelkersam, the Commander of these Brandenburgers, himself a Balt and a descendant of the Russian Admiral Foelkersam who fell at Tsuschima, immediately realized the danger and with great presence of mind shouted to the Commissar: 'You won't get much change out of that chap—he's an Armenian.' Whereupon the Commissar at once started to address the 'Armenian' (from Hamburg!) in what, he presumed, was his mother-tongue. There remained but one thing for Foelkersam to do; out came his tommy-gun, and from the hip he shot down the Commissar, thus at the same time giving the signal for general action. In spite of this contretemps the on-slaught was a complete success.

Episodes of a similar nature occurred, of course, again and again; and to cope with them demanded the greatest possible presence of mind and audacity. The individuals who had been detailed to parley with control posts, officers and Commissars, and to arrange for the onwards transit of the lorries had to possess particularly steady nerves and a ready wit to deal with all the unforeseen contingencies which always arose. On the presence of mind and skill of these spokesmen depended not only the success of the enterprise in hand, but also the lives of their comrades.

In the winter of 1940/41 a battalion of ex-Polish soldiers of West Ukrainian origin was raised in the Neuhammer camp near Liegnitz. The companies were formed of men who had received a very thorough military training in the Polish Army and who were selected, with the assistance of the West Ukrainian Organization, from among the prisoners-of-war. Some were members of the Bandera Group while some belonged to various other West Ukrainian organizations. The Ukrainian leader of the battalion was a hard-bitten partisan named Skonprynka, who was later killed in 1951 while leading a Ukrainian rebellion in the vicinity of Kiev. The German Commandant was Lieutenant Albrecht Herzner, the hero of the Jablonka exploit, and Professor Oberlaender was in charge of the political side.

The battalion raised by Abwehr Section II and equipped, unfortunately, in the most deplorable manner, was given the code-name of 'Nightingale', because it had a choir which could have held its own with even the most world-famous of the Cossack choirs; it was attached to the 1st Battalion of the Brandenburg Regiment and marched into the Soviet Union on June 22nd, 1941. In the battle of Lemberg, patrols of the battalion ascertained that mass executions of Ukrainian nationals were being carried out in the city, and the Commander of the two battalions decided to press on into Lemberg itself during the night June 29/30—seven hours before zero hour fixed for the attack by the 1st Mountain Division. On this occasion the Ukrainian battalion distinguished itself greatly; it occupied the wireless station, and thence issued a proclamation announcing the foundation of a free and independent West Ukrainian State.

In the N.K.V.D. prisons of Lemberg they found the corpses of thousands of recently shot Ukrainian fellow-countrymen and, apart altogether from the spirit of freedom which inspired them, this spectacle reinforced their desire to fight and their determination to throw the Russian invader by force out of the whole of the Ukraine. Close on the heels of this West Ukrainian proclamation came a sharply-worded protest from Rosenberg's office, and although the battalion distinguished itself again and again during the ensuing advance, and particularly at the battle of Vinitza, a gradual change of spirit began to appear. The newly formed Ministry for Eastern Territories had detached the West Ukraine, the districts, that is, of Przemysl and Tarnopol, from the State envisaged by the Ukrainian leaders and had incorporated them and their particularly steadfast population in the General Government, as the remnants of the old Polish State were now called. The net result was that the Ukrainian battalion, which had inspired tens of thousands of West Ukrainians in Lemberg to the highest pitch of eagerness to fight, now became itself unreliable, began to mutiny and finally had to be disbanded; an opportunity of vast potentiality was thus irretrievably lost. Captain Oberlaender tried to intervene with Hitler in person, but the Fuehrer interrupted his dissertation with the words: 'You don't know what you're talking about. Russia is our Africa, and the Russians are our niggers.' After this interview Oberlaender reported to the Commandant of the Brandenburg Regiment and declared soberly: 'That, sir, is Hitler's conception, and that, sir, is a conception which will lose us the war.'

Later, still under Abwehr Section II, Oberlaender raised the 'Bergmann' battalion which was recruited from the Caucasian races and rendered good services on the Caucasian front, but when the German retreat from the Caucasus began, it too became untrustworthy. Men of the Bergmann battalion, under the command of Lieutenants Lange and Moritz, dropped from aircraft far behind the Russian front and for some three months took part side by side with armed Caucasian bands in a series of very successful partisan operations.

During the advance in the Caucasus, one company of the Brandenburg Regiment, in captured Russian lorries, attached itself to a retreating Russian column, seized and secured the bridge into Maikop and thus made possible the capture and holding for the time being of an important source of Russian oil.

Another detachment of the Regiment, under that same Lieutenant Baron Foelkersam who had had trouble with the Armenian from Hamburg, slipped through the Russian lines disguised as Russian soldiers, operated very successfully for some weeks behind the Russian front, captured an entire divisional staff intact and later returned safely to the German lines.

The Ukrainians were by no means the only people whose co-operation it was possible to enlist against the Russians. Even before the beginning of the Russian campaign it was very much in the interests of the border States, Estonia, Latvia and

Lithuania, to exchange intelligence information and to conduct their Intelligence activities with Germany largely according to mutually agreed principles. For these peoples, too, it was a terrible disillusionment when Hitler reversed his policy and left them to their fate at the hands of the Russians. The German minority migrated out of the Baltic States, and the Abwehr officer in Estonia saw to it that those persons who had worked with him in the past were given the opportunity of eluding the clutches of the Russians.

Even so, this past collaboration bore fruit during the war against the Soviet Union, as will be seen from the following report from a German officer:

'Before the opening of the Russian campaign there were in Finland a large number of young Estonians, some of whom had been fighting for the Finns as volunteers during the winter campaign of 1939/40, and some who, after the occupation of the Baltic States by Russia, had fled by boat or on foot across the ice to Finland. Many of them hoped that they would live to see the liberation of their country and cast about to find some means of contributing towards it.

'To make use of these forces, a few well-known Estonian officers who had taken refuge in Germany were sent over to Finland to select and train young Estonians for services which were to be purely in the Estonian national interest. At the same time, the German Intelligence stations were particularly interested in Intelligence reports from the Estonian area, and it was therefore decided to call for volunteers suitable for enlistment in the Intelligence Service. The Finns co-operated with enthusiasm; training quarters were made available on the Soko peninsula, some twenty-five miles west of Helsinki, instructors in wireless telegraphy were provided, and a special wireless headquarters was set up to handle the communications when the organization later went into action. The Estonian volunteers were given uniforms and the status of foreign volunteers in the German Wehrmacht.

'When the Russian campaign started on June 21st, 1941, and

the initial successes of the Germans pointed to a rapid occupation of Estonia, swift action had to be taken. The volunteers—some eighty of them—were mobilized, equipped, given a last short course of instruction and sent to the island of Pellinge to learn the elements of seamanship. Transport, in the shape of two patrol vessels, motor boats and fishing smacks, was provided by the Finnish Navy, which also showed the greatest possible interest in the enterprise.

'In planning the transportation, the following factors had to be taken into consideration: the extreme shortness of the summer nights in these northern latitudes: the use of vessels of three distinct speeds (swift motor boats, medium paced patrol vessels and slow-moving fishing smacks): the limitations imposed upon the use of motor boats in the open seas: the necessity of all these vessels of different speeds arriving at their objective simultaneously and at an hour which would enable the vessels themselves to be well on their return journey and out of sight of the Russian coastal batteries by break of day.

'To cope with all these factors, it was decided that the vessels should be divided into three groups, sailing at precisely calculated intervals, with the slow fishing smacks leading, the motor boats in the middle and the patrol vessels bringing up the rear. A rallying point was pin-pointed off the Gulf of Kumna, whence the two motor boats with an advanced guard Commando under two German officers would make for the selected landing-place and, if necessary and possible, form a bridge-head there. Only when this had been accomplished were the fishing smacks with the main body to approach the shore, while the two patrol vessels were to remain on patrol at the entrance of the gulf.

'The first attempt was made on July 5th, but it failed owing to the rough seas which swamped nearly all the boats. The next attempt, on July 7th, was finally crowned with partial success, though it started badly enough. On the way over, the vessels ran into a heavily escorted Russian convoy. The leading group, the motor boats, actually managed to slip unobserved through the convoy, but then turned about for it was assumed that the presence of the convoy had automatically cancelled the whole enterprise. The group of smacks was put off course by the convoy and then through a navigational error steered for the Loksa Gulf instead of the Gulf of Kumna. Here they were attacked by Russian light patrol craft and withdrew.

The group of patrol vessels, which also bumped into the convoy, was challenged by signal by the Russians and ordered to disclose its identity. The group immediately headed westwards, allowed the convoy to go past on its easterly course and then turned back on its own course on the tail of the convoy, but found that the other groups had not arrived. The commander of the whole expedition decided, notwithstanding, to run into the gulf and without further protection to land his party, which consisted of some forty men, under an Estonian colonel. This operation was carried out without incident.

'On July 10th a third attempt was made to land the remaining forty men and two German officers. While crossing the Gulf of Finland, however, the vessels were attacked with gunfire by units of the Russian Fleet and forced to retire. As a result of this incident it had to be assumed that the Russian coastal guards must by now have been fully alerted and would take measures to repel any attempted landings of this nature; and it was therefore decided to abandon the attempt to send in any further forces by the sea route.

'In the meanwhile wireless communication had been established with the original landing party, and arrangements were made to set up a ground organization for the reception of reinforcements by air-drop. Flown over in an ME 111 and a JU 52, the remainder of the party arrived safely by parachute.

'Missions for this group were fixed by Eighteenth Army, and that Army was more interested in the collection of information

M

than in the carrying out of acts of sabotage; the latter, indeed, were viewed with disfavour, for the Army hoped to capture all installations intact. Nor was the Army very enthusiastic about any form of guerrilla warfare, of which the cost in casualties, they thought, would be out of all proportion to its probable achievements.

'Meanwhile the groups which had installed themselves in the interior of Estonia had split up, partly according to plan and partly owing to Russian intervention. One section very quickly gained touch with the German forces advancing from the west and was able to give much valuable information about that portion of the theatre of operations which it had already reconnoitred. Another group operating in the countryside ran into a large unit of so-called Estonian Brothers of the Forest, men who for fear of deportation or arrest had taken to the woods. During a later stage of the operations this group of Brothers under the command of the Estonian Colonel Leithammel, was supplied with food, medicines, arms, etc., by air.

'In this manner temporary contact was established with five independent groups, which reported the results of their reconnaissance by wireless and whose further tactical activities were directed by Headquarters in consultation with the Army Group concerned. One group advanced from the Aegviidu area in the direction of Reval and on its way forward sent in reports regarding enemy reinforcements that were moving up. Another group, which had been dropped to the west of Wesenberg, marched on Narva and very quickly made contact with units of the German Sixteenth Army, which was advancing to the capture of that city. A third group carried out a reconnaissance of the Wesenberg area, with special instructions to remain in close proximity to the Russian Army Group Command and to report its movements.

'In spite of the rapidity of the advance, the stream of reports continued to arrive without interruption, and the work accomplished earned high praise from the Army. This was certainly the first, and perhaps also the only, occasion on which a reconnaissance operation of this nature was undertaken, on the German side, on so large a scale.

'Casualties were comparatively light. All groups succeeded in making their way back to the German lines, and most of the men then volunteered for service with the Wehrmacht. Finally, two groups of the same unit, whose homes were on Osel, were dropped by parachute, and they, too, accomplished the mission entrusted to them.

' "Operation ERNA", as this had been called and which was regarded by the Germans as a reconnaissance in force, acquired a totally different signification in the eyes of the Estonian people. As many of the participants, on completion of the operation, returned to their homes, where they were not slow in recounting their experiences to all and sundry, the story could not be kept secret, and very soon it became the common property of the whole of the Estonian people. Thanks to the fact that the operation had been carried out under German direction and that it was Estonians to whom the privilege of advancing into their own fatherland and striking the first blow for its liberation was given, the directing staff, and particularly the commander himself, won great esteem and confidence in Estonian nationalist circles. These facts were greatly cherished when, later, high German policy rejected the raising of any Estonian units on the grounds that it was not considered desirable to allow the Estonians to participate in the liberation of their country, and consequently to have a legitimate claim to recognition of their services. Confidence in the German Commander of Operation ERNA never wavered, and it was of great value when, as the result of the completely incomprehensible policy adopted by the German civil administration, Estonia gradually became estranged from the Reich. The German Commander, for his part, never abused the confidence of the Estonians and was never the cause of any disillusionment on the part of the Estonian people.'

In spite of all the strenuous endeavours of the Russian Intel-

ligence Service to seal off their country, there remained throughout the whole war a certain number of sources able to obtain
reports from within Russia itself—or who, at all events, claimed
to be able to do so. Probably the most astonishing case is that
of an agent who worked under the name of Klatt.

At the beginning of the war, the Vienna Abwehr station had
at its disposal a large number of excellent agents established
in South-east Europe. Quite a few of them were Jews or individuals of Jewish origin, and it was only with the greatest difficulty that the chief of the station, Count Marogna-Redwitz
succeeded in shielding his employees from the cruel and unwelcome attentions of the Party machine; but succeed he did,
and for a very considerable time.

Far and away the best agent was the man Klatt, who himself
asserted that he was half-Jewish. The material supplied by
Klatt about Russia was always first class, and sometimes it was
downright sensational. His sources of information, on the
other hand, remained cloaked in anonymity to the very end.
For as long as he was able to remain in Sofia, he declared that
his information came by wireless direct from Russia, where, he
asserted, he actually had a collaborator in the wireless section
of the Kremlin itself. But these claims of his could not stand
the test of scrutiny. On days on which he claimed to have
received messages from Russia, the wireless monitoring service
had been able to prove that there had been no wireless communication at all. Nor could he substantiate his claim to have
received information direct from the Soviet Embassy in Sofia.
But Klatt was able to weather even these crises in his career
for Supreme Headquarters repeatedly affirmed that his reports
were of the highest value. About 1943 he shifted the scene of
his activities to Bucharest, where he repeated the same per-
formance. Again and again he announced that he had startling
new sources of information, but once more none of it could be
confirmed.

When Admiral Canaris was removed from office in February
1944, Klatt's position in view of the new set-up of the German

intelligence organization, seemed to become untenable; but once more this astonishingly clever man survived, and not the least of the reasons for his survival was the fact that he could, with every justice, claim that the material he supplied was all but incomparable.

At the end of 1944, determined once and for all to get at the truth, Schellenberg, the Chief of Bureaux Mil and VI of the Security Service (S.D.), instituted a formal inquiry into Klatt's activities; and in this connection two groups of Abwehr officers found themselves in sharp opposition. One group defended Klatt, the other group asserted that he was obviously a Russian agent and was being used to plant information inside the German Intelligence Service; some of the information given would, of course, be true, they said, for only in that way could the Russians convince the German High Command that Klatt was genuine; but when the time came the Russians, through Klatt, would set a proper trap for the Germans. Schellenberg, who always disliked taking a decision on his own responsibility, went to see General Guderian, the Chief of the General Staff, and asked him whether General Headquarters could dispense with the information furnished by Klatt. With him he took a few of Klatt's reports to show the General. Guderian was already well acquainted with these reports and he told Schellenberg officially that to close down this source would be an act of criminal irresponsibility and that Klatt's reports, especially those on the Red Air Force, were quite unique; he added that there was no other agent who was anywhere near as valuable as Klatt.

That seemed to be the saving of Klatt. But now the Vienna station, to which he was subordinated, decided to try and get his contacts into its own hands, and with this in view it attached a lieutenant to Klatt's own office. The lieutenant, apparently, quickly got some insight into what was happening, but how much he actually found out is hard to say; at the beginning of 1945, however, he reported that he had now acquired complete control of Klatt's sources, and on this Klatt was dropped and was handed over to Gestapo Headquarters in Vienna.

The assumption that Klatt was in reality a Russian agent was soon proved to be wrong, for, as the Russian armies came nearer and nearer to Vienna, he moved heaven and earth to get away from the city, even accepting the risk of being thrown into a concentration camp somewhere in the west. In March 1945 he approached his old captain in the Vienna Abwehr station, imploring him to intervene and somehow to get him away before the Russians took the city. One of Schellenberg's officers—without, incidentally, consulting his chief—agreed that Klatt should be moved westwards; at the same time he secretly told the officer who was to accompany Klatt to let him escape on the way. To show his gratitude, Klatt sent the following message to his benefactor:

'In the course of the next few days, a gentleman of Japanese appearance will be arriving at Aspern aerodrome, *en route* for Sweden. Using the password . . . get in touch with him and arrange that in future he should send his material, not to Klatt but to any recipient you care to select.'

The Japanese in question was actually never contacted. But with almost absolute certainty it can be assumed that he was a certain well-known Japanese journalist, who was known to have been working for many years for the Japanese Intelligence Service.

Those who had busied themselves with the case of this Intelligence mystery man now think it probable that Klatt and the Japanese journalist had been acquainted, through their activities in the Balkans, for many years. The Japanese obtained most excellent reports on Russia, which probably came originally from Turkey; these Klatt bought from him and submitted to the Abwehr as his own. Klatt had felt himself compelled to lie about his sources of information because he thought that if he disclosed the truth he would simply be dismissed. He was able to pay his informant well, for not only did he possess considerable means in dollars, but he also engaged in large-scale currency transactions, which brought him in a very solid income. That he did indeed pay for the information he received is proved by the fact that, in disclosing the source, he stated emphatically that the new recipient of reports must henceforth assume full financial responsibility for payment.

Schellenberg, as he later told a fellow-prisoner, believed that this version was correct, and in support of his opinion he quoted examples of cases in which Klatt's reports bore a close resemblance to the official reports of the Japanese Embassy.

The full story of this singularly interesting agent will probably never be known. But the value of his reports was very highly rated by such authorities as Marogna, Canaris, Schellenberg and Guderian, and they must, then, obviously have been of very great importance.

Needless to say, the Russian Intelligence Service was not idle in Germany either before or during the war, and the German counter-espionage organization had to keep its eyes very wide open. The most spectacular case, which has already been referred to in Chapter Five, was that known as the *Rote Kapelle*, or Red Choir. This was the code-name given by the Abwehr to the major Russian network of agents within Germany, the occupied territories and such neutral countries as Sweden and even Switzerland.

Although the Abwehr was, of course, well aware that the Russians had for many years had agents inside Germany, and though masses of Russian agents were continually being infiltrated or parachuted into the Eastern territories (where, owing to poor training, they were usually picked up almost at once), the scope and size of their high-level espionage activities came as a startling surprise.

After weeks and months of that constant, detailed, unspectacular work which constitutes the vast bulk of all counterintelligence, the Abwehr at last succeeded, during the night of December 12th, 1941, in laying their hands on an important Russian short-wave transmitter in Brussels. This provided the key to what is believed to have been the Russians' chief espionage network, though it was not until a second transmitter, also in Brussels, was captured in the summer of 1942 that its threads were firmly in the hands of the Abwehr. They led to some startling places, to the Air Ministry, the Foreign Office and the Ministry of Economics. In all of these, but particularly in the Air Ministry, Russian agents—Germans, of course, mostly Communists working specifically for the Russians as spies and not simple enemies of the Nazi regime— were active. They were second rank officials and junior staff officers (Canaris' suspicion that even bigger fry, such as Bormann, may have been implicated has never been substantiated), but the value of the information that they were in a position to pass to Moscow was enormous. They had been active for years beneath the very noses of the Gestapo and of the German internal security services, and had it not been for the technical brilliance of the Abwehr's wireless locaters in Brussels, they might well never have been caught. Ideological traitors, who of course do not regard themselves as such, are very slippery fish indeed, as disclosures in Anglo-Saxon countries since the war have shown. The number of men and women implicated and executed for their part in Rote Kapelle has been given as seventy-eight. The figure, however, is not known for certain, and others have placed it as high as 400. Its unmasking, though incomplete, was perhaps the greatest single coup of Abwehr III; it was certainly among the most spectacular. The story is as follows:

Until the opening of hostilities between Germany and the Soviet Union the Russian espionage organization in German and German-occupied territory had kept very quiet. In the summer of 1941, however, the German radio control service in Berlin informed the Brussels branch of the Abwehr that a short-wave station was on the air regularly each night. The transmitter was believed to be somewhere in the vicinity of the Belgian coast.

Agents had no success whatever in discovering its whereabouts and finally a radio location company of the Abwehr, reinforced by a radio location platoon from the Berlin police force, was put on the job. It was soon apparent that the transmitter was actually in Brussels. The search was thus narrowed and with the aid of the new precision locaters, the so-called *Koffergeräte*, a house in the Rue des Atrébates was pin-pointed. A considerable force of field police, equipped with wire-cutters, pick-locks and other such tools, made a surprise entry about midnight, December 12th/13th, 1941. The two flanking houses were simultaneously occupied. In these latter nothing suspicious was found, but a policeman saw a man escaping over the garden wall at the back. He was soon captured. Meanwhile in the central house the police had entered a small, brightly lit room on the first floor. Here they found the transmitter, turned on and ready to transmit, a sure sign that the operator had been taken by surprise while actually at work. Beside the apparatus were various messages, in cipher, and operational instructions. Preliminary interrogation of the captured man revealed that he was a Russian lieutenant, but it proved impossible to decipher the messages.

In the same house a woman was arrested who, according to the papers she carried, was a Parisian. She refused to answer any questions. But a search of her room revealed a secret door, behind which the police discovered a workshop fully equipped for the production of forged papers and documents, both civilian and military.

Another woman was arrested in this house. She was a Jewess by the name of Vera; a victim of racial persecution and of domestic tragedy, she had fallen into the clutches of the Russian agents. From her a certain amount of information was forthcoming. In particular she said that two of the passport-type photographs found in the forger's workshop were pictures of the 'Grand Chef' and of the 'Petit Chef'. But who these men were, she could not say. The Russian Secret Service never allowed its agents any knowledge of their superiors.

177

Among the captured papers were detailed instructions for the use of the transmitter, together with a description of the apparatus, both in German. There were also a quantity of picture postcards from various German towns, notably Berlin, Nuremberg, Augsburg and Hamburg. Abwehr III F, which was responsible for combating foreign espionage, reached the conclusion that German citizens, if not German officials, were connected with the espionage organization. This suspicion of treason was reinforced by Vera's statement that German was the language spoken by the individuals who had frequented this house. This, as may be imagined, caused considerable perturbation at Abwehr Headquarters in Berlin.

In the spring of 1942 news came from Berlin that a new transmitter, probably also located in Brussels and operating on the same wavelength as the other, was once again broadcasting to Moscow. As had been the case with the captured one, hours of transmission were from midnight to 5 a.m. With the help of the radio locaters, this one too was found. During the night of May 19th/20th the field police entered the house. They discovered the transmitter on the ground floor, but the room was deserted. The operator had fled. However, policemen posted in the street saw a man escaping over the roof. When he reached the last row of houses he jumped through a glass roof. After a brief search he was found hiding in the cellar. Under interrogation he revealed that he was called Wilhelm Schwarz, that he came from Koenigsberg in East Prussia, and that until 1934 he had been a leading official of the German Communist Party. Police records confirmed his statements: Schwarz was on the list of 'wanted' men. He had gone to Moscow in 1934, where he had been trained for his job in Belgium.

In his brief-case the interrogating officer found further messages in cipher, the cipher being a numerical one. He also had unciphered messages in German, in his possession. One of these contained a complete Berlin address. Others *en clair* gave detailed information concerning the forthcoming German operations against Stalingrad and the Caucasus—operations which, incidentally, were not launched until the end of the following month. On these papers was a note to the effect that they were on no account to be allowed to fall into German hands; for only four persons in the highest German military positions knew about the plans, and their capture must therefore immediately compromise the source.

The captured documents were flown to Berlin. A brief conference with Admiral Canaris resulted in a decision to inform the heads of the armed services. The Berlin address was revealed to be that of a Luftwaffe officer. He was a Lieutenant Schulze-Boysen, who worked at the Command Staff of the Attaché Department with the O.K.W.

Shortly before the National Socialists had come to power, Schulze-Boysen had been connected with a stenographer who was under suspicion of the police for political reasons. Nothing definite had been proved against him, however. Then, through his fiancée, a granddaughter of Prince Eulenburg, he had succeeded in establishing contact with Goering, who was impressed by his ability. He became a lecturer on political matters. This enabled him to get to know many young people who fell under the spell of his attractive and charming manner. His abnormal way of life attracted others. When the war began he succeeded in placing two of his young people in a cipher unit. Owing to the nature of their employment these two had first-hand knowledge of the work of foreign intelligence services. They passed on everything of interest to Schulze-Boysen and he forwarded all vital information thus acquired to the Russians.

When these young persons learned of the Brussels discoveries, one of them immediately informed Schulze-Boysen by telephone. He at once collected all the incriminating material on which he could lay his hands and arranged, successfully, for its removal to safe keeping in Stockholm. He maintained contact with his people through a secret line to the cipher unit. This line was connected with a telephone in an empty office. Not knowing that his office had recently become occupied by an officer, Schulze-Boysen rang the number. The officer answered, Schulze-Boysen immediately excused himself, saying that he must have got the wrong number, but the suspicions of the officer were aroused. He made a report: the young people were shadowed: and they were arrested when next they met with Schulze-Boysen, as was he.

A member of the Foreign Office was also found to be an active Russian agent and arrested. Finally a considerable number of short-wave transmitters were discovered in various German cities.

Through the information supplied by Vera, in Brussels, the Abwehr got on the track of a firm which was run by the 'Petit Chef' and which did business with German service organizations. It was alleged that the 'Petit Chef' was a Portuguese by the name of Vincenz Corella. He was in the import-export business, had contracts to supply goods to the Wehrmacht in Belgium and thus was entitled to use the international telephone, telegraph and postal services. He could thus ring persons in neutral countries. He was also enabled to visit Denmark and Czechoslovakia 'on business'. It subsequently transpired that the 'Petit Chef' was a Russian captain.

Meanwhile the search for the 'Grand Chef' went on. With Vera's help a forger and his mistress were arrested; the forger was believed to be in touch with the 'Grand Chef'. This forger, who was known as 'the manufacturer', turned out to be a criminal. His sole interest was to make as much money from his craft as he could, regardless of the purpose for which his forgeries might be wanted. The field police therefore offered him a handsome sum to betray his former employer. He had no hesitation in accepting. His first move was to write a letter to an alleged rubber salesman, with whom he had been previously in touch. In this letter he apologized for having failed to keep an appointment and proposed a new meeting. This letter was forwarded by the 'manufacturer's' mistress. Two days later the reply came, suggesting a rendezvous in a Brussels market, but neither this nor a subsequent appointment was kept by the rubber salesman.

A Belgian policeman, who was regarded as trustworthy by the Abwehr, also enjoyed the confidence of the Russian spies. One day the 'manufacturer' approached this policeman with the request that he supply him with blank identity cards, available to him in his job. The policeman, after consultation with the Abwehr, agreed to do so, but insisted that he be supplied with the photographs of the persons for whom the identity cards were wanted. The first photograph was supplied at once. He took it to the Abwehr, who re-photographed it before returning it and the forged card to the policeman. It showed a hitherto unknown young man, aged twenty-five to thirty, with blond hair. Although the face was equally unknown to the other German police authorities, the 'manufacturer' maintained that this was the new head of the Russian espionage organization in Brussels. The Belgian policeman now informed the 'manufacturer' that he would only deliver the forged card to the actual man purporting to be the person to whom it referred, and proposed a meeting-place. To this the 'manufacturer' strangely enough agreed. The young man appeared at the proper place and time and was arrested. But he quite refused to answer any questions either about himself or his contacts. The radio operator, Schwarz, however, maintained that this young man was indeed the Brussels head of the Russian Secret Service.

Meanwhile the search for the 'Grand Chef' continued, and a new clue was being followed up. The 'manufacturer' reported that the Brussels spies, taking alarm, had fled to Paris. The Abwehr therefore began a watch on those persons who frequented German service organizations in that city. The building in the Champs Elysées which housed the administrative headquarters of the Todt Organization soon attracted their attention. People were constantly entering and leaving it without being subjected to any effective security screening. A firm in Brussels was found to have regular dealings with the Todt

Organization. The Wehrmacht liaison officer knew the head of this firm by sight. When shown the photograph of the wanted man believed to be the 'Grand Chef' he confirmed that that man was indeed the head of the firm. Thus the Abwehr was now close on the heels of the 'Grand Chef'. However it was quickly discovered that the liaison officer had no record of the man's address. All attempts to discover it remained fruitless and no further progress was made until an employee of the Brussels firm revealed that his boss had asked him to recommend a dentist a few days before and was indeed going to him for treatment. Inquiries with the dentist confirmed this: the man had an appointment a few days hence. He was actually arrested in the dental chair. But when interrogated he refused to reveal his true identity, and since he persevered in this refusal he continued to be known, and was indeed addressed, as 'Grand Chef'. He did admit that he had been born in Russian Poland. He spoke perfect German, English and French in addition to his native tongue and had been engaged on secret missions abroad, for the Russians, since 1925 or 1926. As time went on it was gradually possible to reach, through him, some of his active fellow-spies. This was achieved by the expedient of leaving him more or less at large and free to move about, though under the constant supervision of two officials. It was due to the carelessness of these guards that he succeeded in making his escape. Although their orders were that two men were to be with him at all times, one day a single guard agreed to accompany him to a chemist's shop where he wished to make a purchase. The shop was very full and the 'Grand Chef' suddenly vanished into the crowd. All attempts to recapture him proved vain.

Thanks to the captured transmitters and ciphers, now broken, the Abwehr succeeded for some time in maintaining contact with Moscow. This proved a most useful source of information. The Abwehr even succeeded in asking Moscow for money, in English currency, allegedly to pay agents, and in due course this arrived, via Sofia.

But this game could not, of course, be kept up for long. Meanwhile the struggle to destroy Rote Kapelle, with its many tentacles stretching across all Europe, continued. It was never finally concluded, and there can be no doubt that that same organization, perhaps in some cases employing the very same men, is still active to-day.

8

The Far East

In the first chapter of this book I have spoken of the German attempts, at the time when the Russians were their allies, to embroil the Soviets with Britain and France in the western parts of Asia. These came to nothing. But at the same period the prospects of causing the British trouble in India and Afghanistan were discussed with them. Here the Russians were more co-operative; however, while approving the German idea, they refused themselves to take any part in plans to foment unrest in those areas.

The first target was Afghanistan, long a thorn in the side of the British Raj, and the aim was the overthrow of the pro-British King and the restoration of Amanulla, then an exile in Rome, to his former throne. Had this project succeeded, it would undoubtedly have led to considerable unrest in India, particularly among the Wazirs, Mohmands, Afridis and other tribes of the North-west Frontier. The initial steps towards the implementation of these plans were to be taken by Haji Mirza Ali Khan, the Faqir of Ipi. The National Socialist Party was at first enthusiastic in support of this, and its representative with the Abwehr planning staff was at this time a certain Habicht, who had played a big part in Austrian affairs.

However political difficulties soon began to be felt. Molotov had second thoughts. He decided that the Afghan venture would not fit in with Russian policy, particularly as he thought that Russia would probably be asked to furnish arms and ammunition—and that she would not do. On the German side, too, Rosenberg viewed this intimate Russo-German *rapprochement* with grave misgivings, and as both the Foreign Office and Canaris himself also regarded with extreme scepti-

185

cism Habicht's 'Indian Fairy Tales', the original large-scale idea was dropped.

But the plan to foment unrest among the anti-British tribes on the North-west Frontier was further pursued by the Abwehr, regardless of the Afghan question. In 1938, the Faqir of Ipi had caused the British many a headache. They had bombed villages in which they believed he and his adherents were living, and they had sent two punitive expeditions against him. By means of artificially caused landslides, ambushes among the inaccessible rocks and so on, a type of warfare in which these mountaineers were experts, they successfully defended themselves against the British. During the war contact with the Faqir of Ipi had been maintained by the Italian Consul in Kabul; but now the Abwehr was anxious to establish a direct link with him. A scholar of international repute, well acquainted from previous expeditions with the country and the people, was sent out. This expedition, however, ended in tragedy, for the German emissary was shot dead by Afghan gendarmes and his companion was left, grievously wounded, before ever they reached their destination. Later the Afghans declared that they had taken these foreigners, disguised in the costumes of the country, to be emissaries of Amanulla.

The Indian plans entered on a new phase when the Indian nationalist leader, Subhas Chandra Bose, arrived in Berlin in 1941. In the spring of 1941 he had crossed the Russo-Afghan frontier, accompanied by a German road engineer who was in Afghan employ and who had previously held an important position in the Todt Organization. In Moscow no official cognizance had been taken of his presence, but the Russians had done everything they could to make his stay there a pleasant one. Revolution in India fitted their plans excellently.

While in Moscow Bose had an interview with the German Ambassador, Count von der Schulenburg, whose profound knowledge of Asia impressed him greatly; he referred to this repeatedly in his subsequent conversations with Admiral Canaris.

In Germany, Bose devoted himself with great energy to political propaganda and to the recruitment of supporters from among Indian prisoners-of-war, most of whom had either been captured or had deserted in the African theatre of operations. A considerable number were persuaded to take up arms against Britain; they were formed into an Indian Legion under German leadership, and were given a thorough course of training. These Indian Legionaries were issued German uniforms with an armband of the Indian national colours. The Sikhs, as a strict caste apart, retained their turbans. The differences in religious and caste customs caused the German supply services endless headaches, both in the quartering and the feeding of these men. Separate cooking arrangements had to be made for Hindus and Moslems; common use of the same water supply was unthinkable; and if so much as the shadow of a Moslem fell by chance across the cooking-pots of a Hindu sepoy, the latter was compelled to leave his food untouched.

On one occasion a Sikh, in a spirit of progress, allowed himself to be shorn of his long hair and beard; that same night he was shot in his sleep by his brother Sikhs. The German Commandant, a man of Austrian origin, pretended to accept the given explanation of suicide, for he realized that any investigation of this crime inspired by religious fanaticism was bound to be misunderstood by the Sikhs.

In military training, commands were given in German, but instruction was conducted in English, the lingua franca of all Indian soldiers of the British Indian Army. The Indian soldiers proved themselves to be particularly skilful in single combat, and as scouts, and the warlike Sikhs, for whom the British had always shown a preference both in the army and the police service, possessed all those excellent attributes required to fit them into the pattern of the German armed forces.

Subhas Chandra Bose showed the greatest possible interest in the military training of his adherents. Selected individuals were attached to the Abwehr for instruction in sabotage and subversive activities. While the Germans still cherished dreams of a thrust through the Caucasus and on as far as the Persian Gulf, their intention was to send the Indian legionaries out by air to start a general uprising in India. But Bose insisted that his co-operation in the organization for the liberation of India must be dependent on the world situation. In his sober appreciation of the possibilities he resembled Admiral Canaris; the latter knew that Bose never talked wildly, and valued him all the more for it. Bose was in no way a collaborator, in the evil sense which the word has acquired of recent years; rather he was a true Indian patriot with but one idea, who was prepared to do nothing simply for Germany's sake, but anything and everything, including the harnessing of German interests, for India.

In the late autumn of 1942 he said to Canaris: 'You know as well as I do that Germany cannot win this war. But this time victorious Britain will lose India. Even the British will not be able to break their promise to give up their dominion over India, a promise made of their own free will in 1940.' When Bose realized that Germany had nothing more to offer him in the way of an advanced base in any of its theatres of war for his fight to free India, he got in touch with the Japanese, who were in a position to give him more assistance in the implementation of his political plans. Oshima, the Japanese Ambassador, obtained the acquiescence of the German authorities to Bose's departure. In February 1943 he boarded the German U-190 and was taken over by a Japanese submarine in the middle of the Indian Ocean. From Japan he went to Burma, and in June 1943 he crossed the Indo-Burman frontier with a small Indian Army of Liberation and some Japanese units; after the collapse of Germany he was still waging jungle warfare against the British.

According to an official report, he crashed over Formosa while on a flight to Japan in a Japanese military aircraft. Later reports claim that he is now in China, but they do not appear to merit any credence.

After his departure, Bose's adherents in Germany found

themselves without a leader. In 1944/45 they were employed on anti-aircraft duties and as coastal patrols on quiet portions of the western front. Some of them finally succeeded in returning to India, and when the indian Prime Minister, Pandit Nehru, solemnly unfurled the flag of independent India in New Delhi in August 1947, among the many Indian soldiers present were some of the former brothers-in-arms of the nationalist leader, Subhas Chandra Bose.

The ever-increasing intensity of the economic war in the Atlantic, and its extension to all the seas, including the Antarctic, led, in the spring of 1940, to an examination of the possibility of attacking the enemy war economy in the Pacific.

From Japanese sources reports were received that wolfram and other strategically important raw materials were being shipped in increasing quantities from East Asiatic ports in British and neutral ships to Britain. The ports most actively engaged were stated to be Shanghai, Canton, Manila and the Straits Settlements ports. Attempts to strike at this trade by means of submarines operating off the African coast had on the whole proved fruitless. To press forward as far as the China seas was beyond the capabilities of the U-boats since their radius of action was not great enough for such far-flung enterprises.

But in the years during which Germany still maintained friendly relations with the Soviet Union, a very tempting way for the unobtrusive transfer of commerce raiders to the Pacific presented itself, namely the North-east Passage through the Bering Straits into the vast open spaces of the Pacific itself. Japan's benevolent attitude strengthened the feasibility of the plan, for the successful execution of which there were two essential pre-requisites—first, the raiders had to be got through the North-east Passage completely camouflaged and unobserved; and secondly, once there, they had to be adequately supported in the Pacific itself and furnished with constant information on alterations to the sea-routes as a result of the war situation, on the density of enemy shipping in the various areas, and on the various air and wireless security measures introduced by the enemy.

Before the outbreak of war, a tentative liaison had been established, at the instigation of Admiral Canaris, between the Abwehr and the Japanese Naval Intelligence Service. But the general world situation in the 1930s was such that there seemed to be but little likelihood of Germany's being able to wage a cruiser war on commerce in the Pacific within the foreseeable future. Now, however, the German Intelligence Service had to establish itself in the shortest possible space of time on the Asiatic continent and there organize a comprehensive reconnaissance of the Pacific Ocean. Accordingly instructions were issued to an officer of the Abwehr directing him to establish as rapidly as possible an intelligence network in the ports of the Pacific, from which continuous and timely information on the movements of shipping could be sent via Abwehr Headquarters in Berlin to the Naval High Command. In this connection, partly out of deference for Japan's neutrality, and partly on account of the growing tension between Japan and the United States, and also to avoid exposing Japan to the charge of having aided Germany's war in the Pacific, the Japanese Intelligence Service was not to be involved.

When asked to whom he proposed to entrust the task of creating a Far Eastern intelligence service in the middle of a war and in the face of an extremely difficult political situation in East Asia, Admiral Canaris selected an ex-naval officer of the first war who, though he had never served in the Far East, had been a business man in the Middle East and had shown that he was just the right type to cope with an exceptional task in exceptional circumstances. The choice proved to be a most happy one. The officer concerned has given the following account of his activities:

'For the establishment of an intelligence network, the heterogeneous, four-zone city of Shanghai was the ideal centre. In it shipping interests of great magnitude and importance were concentrated; even during the war years ships under every flag that sails the seven seas found their way to Shanghai, for in Shanghai they could find all that they required in the way of provisions, repair facilities and equipment. Apart from this, the city's inhabitants in 1940 included people of almost every nation, and this offered a particularly wide choice in the selection of agents suitable for the obtaining and passing on of information. The most fertile fields for the intelligence officer's purposes were the International Concession, which forms the heart of the city, and the Japanese, Chinese and French concessions (for the Shanghai French were in general supporters of the Vichy Government). On the other hand, the very heterogeneity of the city imposed upon an intelligence officer the utmost caution and demanded of him a shrewd judgment of human nature and the ability to put his finger on the real reason why any particular agent offered his services.

'In the event, we succeeded in a comparatively short time in reconnoitring and almost completely covering the whole shipping on the Wang Poo and Yang Tse Kiang. But wireless communication over the great distances from Shanghai to Berlin was at first beset with many technical difficulties. In accordance with the pre-arranged plan, a first-class wireless operator was sent out on demand by Abwehr Headquarters. Because of his cover story, he was not able to bring his apparatus with him, and when at last the valuable instruments did arrive in Shanghai, they were found to have been smashed to bits in transit. At first we tried to get the necessary spare parts locally, but here again we had to proceed with the utmost caution, lest the enemy intelligence services should get any inkling of our activities. In the end we were forced to ask Berlin to send us the more valuable of the components, and in due course they arrived; but in the meanwhile we had wasted the results of a whole month's activity owing to lack of means of communication.

'Once a communication link had been established with the Abwehr Belzig station, it worked with complete smoothness, proved capable of handling the constantly increasing load of traffic placed upon it and was obviously a source of very considerable satisfaction to all concerned.

'An extension of our field of reconnaissance called for further bases—in Tientsin and Canton, for example—and if possible for a penetration into shipping activities of the Philippines and around the Australian coast. The places on which our organizational activities were next concentrated were Tientsin and Tsing Tao, and in both we succeeded in setting up an efficient intelligence service in direct and continuous communication with Shanghai.

'Reconnaissance of the ports on the South China coast proved a much harder task. Any penetration and observation of the trade and shipping movements from Canton, Hong Kong and other such ports were particularly difficult. A personal visit to them by a German Intelligence officer was not possible, for the Sino-Japanese conflict barred the land route, and since a British cruiser had stopped a Japanese liner on the high seas between San Francisco and Kobe, and had removed from her a number of Germans of military age, passage on Japanese vessels had been forbidden.

'Intelligence liaison between Shanghai and Canton could therefore be organized only on a restricted scale and through middle-men. Much of the information received in this way from Canton was valueless, because of the inevitable delay in its transmission. To improve the situation I decided myself to try and get to Canton via Nankin, in spite of the war. But I was forced to abandon the attempt while still short of Nankin, as the Japanese military authorities would not tolerate the presence of any foreigner in the operational zone. To disguise myself as a Chinaman was, alas, not possible; my skin was not at all of the right colour, nor my eyes the proper shape!

'Looking back I feel justified in claiming that the information sent by our organization to Naval High Command contributed in no small measure to the very considerable amount of damage done to enemy shipping in the Pacific Ocean. It was thanks to us that an auxiliary cruiser, which had successfully made the trip through the North-east Passage, received timely information of important events in the Pacific and was able, among other things, to slip unobserved through the enemy's lines of communication and to lay minefields off various Australian ports, which caused great damage to the enemy's shipping and a very effective dislocation of his normal sailing schedules.

'Our observation of enemy maritime methods in the Pacific also gave us a valuable insight which enabled us to draw conclusions on the convoy system employed in the Atlantic and on the methods of concentration of convoys off the African coast. In the Pacific ships normally sailed independently and made for a previously fixed rendezvous, where they would form convoy for the further journey to the British Isles.

'In this way, the Shanghai station operated a service whose effectiveness reached as far as the submarine war in the Atlantic.

'The outbreak of war between Japan and the United States in December 1941 put an end to the activities of the Shanghai station, in so far as German naval operations in the Pacific were concerned. But the station which, by the end of 1941, had been very considerably expanded, continued to function with a new staff and on fresh tasks dictated by the changed conditions, right up to the end of the war.'

9

Admiral Canaris

THE Abwehr was so very much the creation of Admiral Canaris that I feel I cannot do better than close this book with a chapter about him. When he took over, in 1935, it was a small though efficient unit. When he was removed, in the spring of 1944, its great days of achievement were over. The political struggle with the Nazi Party, anxious to gain control of every sort of intelligence activity, had then been lost. This attempted usurpation of military intelligence by a fundamentally political organization had been one of the major factors in limiting the efficiency of the German Secret Service, and had therefore caused considerable damage to the whole German war effort. Once Canaris had gone, the Abwehr soon began to disintegrate until by the end of the war it was only a shadow of its former self while the Nazi S.D., using methods which to Canaris were anathema attempted with only partial success to fulfil the functions ,of an intelligence service.

Thus Canaris, during the more important years, besides controlling a world-wide network of intelligence stations and their ancillary services, besides having to outwit the British, French, American and Russian Intelligence Services, had yet also to engage in a steady if largely silent struggle with enemies and rivals at home, anxious to usurp his position and hence his power. This surely makes his achievements all the more remarkable.

Wilhelm Canaris, the son of an industrialist, was born in Aplerbeck, near Dortmund, in 1887. The Canaris family had migrated to Germany in the seventeenth century from Sala on Lake Como; it did not originate, as has been generally supposed, in Greece, although Canaris is the name of one of

Greece's naval heroes, who earned fame in the war which liberated his country from the Turkish yoke, and the German Admiral kept a picture of this Greek hero, wearing his cap with its liberation badge, hanging in his own home.

Wilhelm Canaris entered the Imperial German Navy on April 1st, 1905. He was present at the battle fought by Graf von Spee's squadron off the South American coast and was interned with his fellow-survivors. He succeeded in making his escape and, overcoming all difficulties, he made his way back to Spain. He reported to the German authorities there, and was given employment in the intelligence section; he was entrusted with the task of purchasing stores and commodities which were in short supply in the Reich and arranging for their transportation by circuitous route to Germany.

Later he returned to Germany and entered the submarine service. In the spring of 1918 he was given command of a U-boat, which he sailed, via the Atlantic and through the Straits of Gibraltar, into the Adriatic. There he made war on enemy commerce; among his brother officers were Arnauld de la Ferrière and Martin Niemoeller. With the collapse of the Austro-Hungarian monarchy, the German submarines returned, after a hazardous journey, to their base in Kiel.

In Kiel red flags already flew at the mastheads of the battle-ships. The revolution had begun, the war was over. The new German republic was soon engaged in a desperate struggle for survival; peace conditions, which were in any way tolerable, had to be obtained from the Allies, while in the Eastern territories there was open war against the forces of militant communism.

By tradition and conviction Canaris was a confirmed monarchist, and it was during this period that he developed that implacable opposition to communism which marked the rest of his life. This basic tenet of his political outlook sheds considerable light on his subsequent attitude towards National Socialism. On the one hand he recognized the National Socialists as the enemies of communism, and as such he welcomed them cordially; on the other, and in an increasing measure as time passed, he thought he saw in the influential circles of the Nazi leaders the seeds of a species of national bolshevism which might blossom forth as downright communism, and on this account he distrusted and feared them. In the midst of war he viewed with the deepest concern the situation revealed by the exposure of the Rote Kapelle, the Soviet Intelligence organization which had installed itself in the German Air Ministry; he firmly believed that the threads of this organization stretched outwards and upwards to Hitler's own Headquarters and to his deputy, Martin Bormann, himself.

Throughout the 1920s and early 1930s he was promoted in the normal way. He was already in command of a cruiser of the modest fleet which was allowed to Germany under the Versailles Treaty, and in 1934 was to have been appointed Commandant of the fortress of Swinemuende. At an age when he could still look forward to many years of activity, this appointment would have meant the end of his active career and a long evening of life spent in semi-retirement. But at that moment disagreements led to the removal of the naval Captain Patzig from his post as Chief of Abwehr in the German Ministry of Defence. The appointment was given to Canaris who was thus saved from the inactivity which had threatened him.

It was an appointment admirably suited to his capabilities and gifts. It was not just a coincidence that so many naval officers were to be found in the Abwehr Service. Foreign reconnaissance demands a knowledge of other countries, or a long period of training for those who do not possess such knowledge. In the army few officers had the opportunity of foreign travel or of protracted service abroad, whereas in the navy foreign tours of duty formed a normal and important part of an officer's career.

On assuming this new appointment Canaris found an organization which had already been functioning well for a decade

197

and a half and which had been built on the principle of decentralization. The Central Office gave general instructions and retained in its own hands the study of such branches of activity as were of general application, such as the technical aspect, the organization of wireless communications, secret codes, and ciphers. It very rarely exercised any direct control over agents; this was done almost entirely by the various Abwehr stations and, in wartime, by the War Organizations in friendly and neutral countries.

The sum of money available for the Intelligence Service, which had to be found from the very small budget of the Hundred Thousand Man Army, had been of very modest proportions; the Abwehr was thus forced to abandon any idea of widespread and costly activity abroad, and to concentrate instead on specific and precisely defined objectives; and in accordance with the principle of decentralization, heavy responsibility was placed on the Abwehr stations. The corollary of this was that great confidence was reposed in them.

To this system Admiral Canaris adhered, and the foundation of his success is to be found in the careful manner in which he selected his subordinates and the trust he placed in them. In this respect he proved to be a master, although it is open to doubt whether the conventional phrase, a good judge of men, can with justice be applied to him. He sometimes made mistakes and he placed too much confidence in men to whom he had assigned certain duties. There are two sorts of confidence —confidence in the mental capability of the individual to carry out the task entrusted to him; and confidence in the character and integrity of the man in whom trust is reposed. A mistake in the former, and it was here that Canaris occasionally went wrong, can be easily remedied; but an error of judgment in the latter is dangerous, and in this Canaris rarely if ever made a mistake.

The reward of his trust was the loyalty and confidence which his officers and subordinates felt for him. Of his capabilities they had no doubts, for he was a man of many gifts and of keen, swift-working intelligence; and in the man himself they could safely place their trust, for they knew that he would never abandon them if ever they found themselves in difficulties. The intelligence officer is continually face to face with dangerous situations and difficult decisions. And in the Third Reich, in addition to these normal hazards, everyone, without exception, who was engaged in intelligence work and who had any contacts abroad, was subjected to the constant suspicious observation of the Gestapo and the Security Service. If one of his officers ever got into difficulties with these latter people, he knew he could still count on the solid suppor tof Admiral Canaris.

The Admiral has sometimes been portrayed as a Mystery Man, and it is possible that, consciously or subconsciously, he contributed to the growth of this legend. It gave him the great advantage of being left alone and unpestered by people. He was, as no one who came in contact with him could fail to recognize, very highly strung; and he was obviously determined to avoid all irrelevant trivialities and details, for only by so doing could he meet the immense demands made upon his ingenuity and determination, and preserve his energy and his comprehensive grasp of the vast field of activity which had been entrusted to him. There is a saying of the philosopher Lichtenberg, which aptly fits Canaris. 'One should not,' he wrote, 'say "I am thinking", but rather, just as one says "it is raining", one should say "it is being thought" '; that exactly applies to Canaris. 'It'—thought—was independently at work within him. When some new problem was submitted to him, he did not think it over, but let it simmer independently within himself, and he could be sure that a suitable solution would occur to him; and this 'occurrence' of a solution is the practical manifestation of Lichtenberg's theory.

Canaris, as were his officers, was a man rich in intuition. Both he and they had to feel confident that in the ever-changing pattern of events the right idea would eventually strike them; and when a chief finds himself working with men of vision and imagination who are at the same time officers, men bred upon discipline and accustomed both to obey orders and to have their own orders implicitly obeyed, then there is welded a combination of personal and official relationships such as is to be found nowhere else. It was just this human relationship, this mixture of military attitude, mutual respect for intelligence and efficiency and a wholesome measure of personal admiration and affection, which constituted the backbone of the Service under Admiral Canaris. This feeling that they were secure, I would almost say that they were under superhuman protection, was never lost by those who stood close to him.

Human decency was the guiding principle on which he worked and upon which he insisted that his officers also should work. On the conclusion of the Sosnovski case, he and some of his officers were discussing the various facts which had come to light. Sosnovski, said the Admiral suddenly, had used the true love of one woman and the credulity of many women to further his own purposes, and that was a thing which no Abwehr officer must do, permit or cause to be done. There may be some who think that sentiments of this nature find no place in the framework of an intelligence service. They are wrong, as the Sosnovski case proves. The excellent report on German mobilization which he sent to the Polish General Staff was dismissed in Warsaw as being false information. The Polish Intelligence Service was hoodwinked by a falsified report played into their hands by the Germans; and when Sosnovski returned to his own country he was charged with having supplied false information and even with having willingly collaborated with the Germans in its preparation, and was flung into prison.

If an intelligence service is conducted on the lowest ethical plane, it cannot expect to enjoy the confidence of its superiors, and the whole organization, sickly from top to bottom, is an unclean entity. The Abwehr under Canaris was a clean and healthy body. Only thus could it within four and a half short years have become such an efficient intelligence service; its efforts cleared the way for the armies invading Poland and France of all those obstacles (ignorance of the enemy's forces, their composition and distribution), which might have barred their path, and its flexibility was such that it could immediately grapple with new tasks in Denmark, in Norway and in the Balkans.

When, as the result of the Russo-German Pact, the Russians occupied the Baltic States, the members of the intelligence services of these countries found themselves in grave and immediate danger. There could be no doubt that the Russians would seize everybody who had been employed in intelligence work against the Soviet armed forces. Canaris' representative in Estonia collected the members of the Intelligence Branch of the Estonian General Staff, supplied them with the necessary cover and shipped them safely to Stettin. Confident that this action would meet with his chief's approval, it was only after he had accomplished it that he made any report to the Admiral. Canaris not only approved; he did much more. He personally assumed responsibility for the housing and future financial security of these officers. In contrast to this the confidential agents of certain of the Allied powers were abandoned without help and fell into the hands of the Russians.

Such episodes did not remain hidden from the members of other intelligence services all over the world, nor were they isolated cases. When Moruzow fell into disfavour in Rumania, Canaris did his best to help him, and many are the men who owe much to the Admiral's helping hand.

What, in reality, does an intelligence service aim at? On one occasion, when I was with the Near East station, I had an interview with a very senior officer of Supreme Headquarters. 'What exactly do you want to know, sir?' I asked. 'Do you wish to find out whether the 3rd Pioneer Battalion of the Free French is in Deir ez Zor or in Aleppo, or are you interested in whether the Turkish generals are for or against Turkey's entry into the war, or what?'

201   O

'We want information,' replied the staff officer, 'on which the High Command can base its operational decisions.'

This is a very happy definition of what must ultimately be the task of an intelligence service. There is a great temptation mechanically to collect any and every sort of information from any odd source, without seriously considering whether the source is reliable or not. Even sources which have been giving good results for a considerable time are apt to have periods of aridity, particularly if the agent concerned is more or less dependent on the rewards he is paid according to quantity of information he brings in; in cases of this sort the officer responsible must have the wit, the honesty and the courage to report when one of his sources begins to weaken: such plain speaking can only increase the mutual confidence between a superior and his subordinates and vice versa.

Canaris' Service was officially charged only with the obtaining of information. The material obtained then went to the General Staff, Section Foreign Armies, East or West, or to Naval or Air Headquarters, where it would be collated and its value assessed. Before the outbreak of war and for the first year or so of war this system worked satisfactorily enough. The confidence placed by the staffs concerned in the efficiency of the Admiral and his officers, and the personal contacts maintained between the men of the General Staff and the Abwehr Offices ensured a successful co-operation. The Intelligence apparatus, however, was very much of a closed circuit; it was also very sensitive, and any major change of personnel was liable to upset its equipose.

This imbalance was more likely to occur when the change of personnel took place on the collating side than when it happened on the supplying side. As the war proceeded, the number of young officers on the General Staff gradually increased very considerably. Now rejuvenation without any doubt is most valuable in many instances, both on the Staff and at the front. But it can easily lead to inefficiency in a branch of the service whose success is dependent upon the training and the experience of its officers. No officer, however young, was ever given a normal General Staff appointment unless he had had adequate staff training; but there was no hesitation in putting young men into the Intelligence Collation and Evaluation Section of the General Staff, who had no knowledge either of foreign countries and their psychological characteristics, or of the technical and routine working of the intelligence service which supplied them with their information.

The young General Staff officer, for instance, who told the head of the Hamburg Abwehr station that his report on the imminent break-out from Brittany southwards was valueless, because it contained no details of the formations participating, was guilty of a piece of bad and stupid evaluation. Information about the enemy is not to be had for the asking; but when a report such as this Hamburg report is sent in, it is the duty of the General Staff officer to draw the logical conclusions, to deduce the probabilities and to act accordingly.

Much the same occurred over the reports on the Sicily landing. In all, about fifty reports were submitted, some of them with details of the intended landing beaches. In some cases the details proved to be correct, in others they were wrong. Complaints from the General Staff followed. It seems to have been completely forgotten by the Staff that, while the enemy makes a plan in the first instance and information about that plan may then be obtainable, not infrequently last minute factors arise which necessitate changes, and by that time either no one is any longer in a position to find out about the changes, or the means of passing on the information, if it has indeed been obtained, no longer exist.

The most important example of this sort of error is furnished by the North Africa landings. The Abwehr correctly reported, not once but repeatedly, the places where the enemy intended to land. The Spanish Intelligence Service confirmed that in their opinion these places were the most probable objectives for such an invasion. Yet the German Embassy in Madrid knew better, as the memoirs of Sir Samuel Hoare, the British

Ambassador, point out; and the ideas of the Embassy carried more weight at Hitler's Headquarters than did the reports of the Abwehr.

This was a telling example of faulty selectivity. While reports from the Military Intelligence Service were read, innumerable other people and departments, involved however indirectly with intelligence matters, were also given an uncritical hearing. Furthermore, Hitler inclined to give more credence to the creations of his own fantasy and wishful thinking than to the facts as acquired by the Abwehr and front-line reconnaissance; and as time went on, his entourage condoned this state of affairs with increasing equanimity, until even his military advisers themselves could not resist the effects of his prophetic utterances.

On the top of all this was the fact that Canaris and his Service were a thorn in the flesh of Himmler and Heydrich. These two had absolute control over internal Intelligence, the Police, the Gestapo and the sources of information which the Security Service had set up for itself abroad. It is true that they had been given a directive limiting their activities to political and police information; but their great ambition was to meddle also in military affairs which is, perhaps, understandable, for in war it is the military affairs which are of paramount importance. Such military information as came their way went, not to the Military Intelligence Service for evaluation or to the General Staff for incorporation in the consolidated picture of the military situation, but direct to Hitler, usually accompanied by a broad hint pointing out how much more efficient the Security Service was than the Abwehr; and neither Himmler nor Hitler had the insight to realize the gravity of the error in selectivity which was thus perpetrated.

Then there were those difficulties which were attributable to the sympathies which some of Canaris' officers felt towards the opposition, and which they had not the skill to keep from the prying eyes of Himmler, Heydrich and the rest.

Colonel (later General) Oster was the Chief of the Central

Office, which was in charge of the technical side, but which had nothing to do with the actual obtaining of information. During the winter of 1939/40 the date of the opening of the Western campaign was postponed several times. Oster was very friendly with the Netherlands Military Attaché, Sas. Early in May 1940 Sas learnt from the Japanese the date finally fixed for the Western offensive. He asked Oster if this were correct, and the latter replied quite spontaneously that it was and that Holland as well as Belgium were to be invaded. Oster, mindful of the manner in which the unprovoked attack on Belgium in 1914 had been the decisive factor in rousing world opinion against Germany, thought that the extension of the war westwards and an onslaught on the neutral Low Countries, far from improving Germany's position, would do the greatest possible harm to the German cause. He assumed that on Sas's report the Queen of Holland and the King of the Belgians would broadcast to the whole world that within forty-eight hours Germany intended to overrun their countries, and that world opinion would therefore cause Hitler once again to hold up his attack and thus give a further opportunity for a peaceful settlement of the conflict. But his expectations were unrealized. After the repeated changes which had already been made in the date for the opening of the Western campaign, neither Holland nor Belgium paid the slightest attention to Sas's reports and Oster's efforts were therefore nullified. Nor were the Dutch defensive measures against a possible German attack strengthened, and so, from this point of view, no harm was done the German troops.

Also in close touch with the resistance movement was an officer of the Abwehr stationed in Rome, Josef Mueller, who through his contacts at the Vatican passed on messages to the Allies, urging them to open negotiations. Oster, his collaborator Dohnany, and Mueller were arrested. Canaris certainly did his best to help these officers of his; but it has never been proved that he was already aware of their activities and, taking everything into consideration, it is extremely unlikely that he was.

Nor have I any reason to believe that Canaris at any time sought or made contact with Germany's enemies, though frequent opportunities for such activity were presented to him. For example, the Russians once proposed to the head of the War Organization, Stockholm, that negotiations might be opened. That officer immediately reported to Berlin in person, and Canaris took him at once to the Foreign Office, that is to say to the proper Government department for dealing with the country's foreign policy. The American approach to von Papen and the Turkish Foreign Minister's suggestion that Archbishop Spellman's help be enlisted to secure peace has been mentioned, and the results described, in Chapter One of this book. Again, in the autumn of 1943 a Hungarian officer informed an Abwehr officer stationed in the Balkans of an approach made by the British, with American backing, to the Hungarian General Staff. As soon as Canaris was informed, he communicated with the Hungarian General Staff and saw to it that the information was passed to the German and Hungarian Foreign Ministers. Such was not the behaviour of a man anxious to establish relations of his own with the enemy.

I have already mentioned the approach made to me, as head of the Istanbul War Organization in April 1944, via the intermediary of certain Turkish friends. I had by then returned to Germany and Admiral Canaris had been dismissed. When I was being interrogated by the Gestapo in July of that year, I spoke of this incident. My interrogator was intensely interested to hear that attempts at establishing contact were being made by the enemy in that quarter. This is hardly surprising, since some of Himmler's officers, and particularly Schellenberg, have repeatedly asserted that Himmler and his colleagues were not only most anxious to open peace negotiations, but had actually already done so behind Hitler's back.

Men without morals tend to assume a similar immorality in others. The Abwehr had, of course, ample opportunity for establishing contact with the enemy. If Himmler was, as seems more than likely, attempting to do this for his own interests, it is not surprising that he should have reacted so violently against the Abwehr. Indeed, the Gestapo officer who interrogated me told me after the war that early in 1944 Himmler had issued instructions for the arrest of Canaris and of all those Abwehr officers who were in his confidence and who had served abroad. They were to go to the concentration camps.

But from none of Canaris' officers serving overseas has there ever been even a suggestion that he called upon them to open peace negotiations, or indeed even to establish contact, directly or indirectly, either with members of hostile intelligence services or with the Government of countries at war with Germany.

In the summary proceedings taken against him before he was murdered in a concentration camp, no accusations of this nature were made against the Admiral. As Headquarters of the Security Service was in possession of all the ciphers used by the Abwehr and had for a long time kept a strict watch on all Abwehr wireless communications, no activity of this nature, had it taken place, could have escaped their notice; and had the Security Service acquired the slightest evidence in this direction, they would have been only too eager to produce it.

For his opponents, then, if they wished to acquire control of the Intelligence Service, there remained no other course but to try and get rid of Canaris by a policy of continually urging Hitler to dismiss him from his post.

The accusations made against the Abwehr in the process are without foundation. They boiled down to the facts that two members of the Istanbul station and one employee of Abwehr Section III deserted to the British, but shortly afterwards the woman secretary of an S.D. officer in Ankara (Moyzisch, the employer of the celebrated spy called Cicero), also deserted to the British, and quite early on a Soviet spy organization was discovered, ensconced in the Air Ministry. These are episodes which are bound to occur in any war, and particularly in a war where world ideologies are in conflict. Meanwhile the serious cases of treachery occurred, not in the Abwehr, but in those circles which, from the National Socialist point of view, were or should have been above suspicion.

As a young man, Canaris had chosen an officer's career and had followed it without remarkable distinction till ripe middle age. His great task, the creation and direction of the Intelligence Service, came to him late in life. He approached it and accomplished it with an open mind and heart, and very quickly the value of his services was to be proven in the test of war. The campaigns in Poland and France showed that all the necessary preliminary reconnaissance had been well and faithfully accomplished; those in Denmark, Norway, in the Balkans and in Russia proved more. They proved that he had created an organization which was capable of dealing swiftly with new tasks, which could improvise on a grand scale, and which, in its knowledge and technique, was the equal of all, and the superior of most, of the enemy intelligence services. The creation of new stations in the Near and Far East at a time when Germany was isolated from the rest of the world, showed that he had selected men for his command who knew how to break through this isolation and bring help to German troops in Africa and to German ships on the farthermost seas. By timely intervention he saved the Rumanian oil, the Wehrmacht's most vital and valuable raw material. He nurtured the pro-German minorities both in Europe and Asia with a firm and understanding hand, and he utilized them to tie down enemy forces and to lighten the heavy burdens placed upon the troops at the front. He created the units which modern war has found to be indispensable—the Brandenburgers, fighting units to whom tasks on all fronts were allotted, tasks which made as many demands on their enterprise and presence of mind as they did on their fighting qualities.

In the nature of things, the work of Canaris and his Service was carried out in the shadows and without publicity. Their accomplishments shared the tragic fate of the great feats of the German soldiers; all was brought to naught by the abysmal inadequacy of the German political and military leadership. It was his particular personal tragedy that Admiral Canaris, with all the knowledge that was at his disposal, was able, perhaps before any one else, to recognize the fateful approach of an inexorable doom.